Cognitive Connections

Multiple Ways of Thinking with Math

R. E. Myers

Illustrated by
Ernie Hager

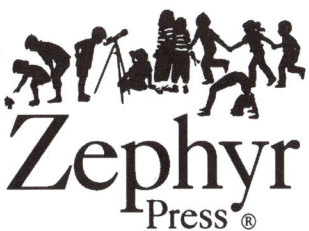

Zephyr Press®

REACHING THEIR HIGHEST POTENTIAL
Tucson, Arizona

To my children—

Ted, Margy, Hal, and Karen—

who inspired much of what follows.

Cognitive Connections
Multiple Ways of Thinking with Math
Grades 4–8
©1996 by Zephyr Press
Printed in the United States of America
ISBN 1-56976-035-7
Editors: Stacey Lynn and Stacey Shropshire
Illustrations: Ernie Hager
Cover Design: Nancy Taylor
Design and production: Daniel Miedaner
Zephyr Press
P.O. Box 66006
Tucson, Arizona 85728-6006

All rights reserved. The purchase of this book entitles the individual teacher to reproduce the forms for use in the classroom. The reproduction of any part for an entire school or school system or for commercial use is strictly prohibited. No form of this work may be reproduced, transmitted, or recorded without written permission from the publisher.

Library of Congress Cataloging-in-Publication Data are available.

Contents

Foreword	vi
Introduction	vii
To the Teacher	xi
Student Activities	1
Numbers	
1. Twos and Threes	2
2. Live Numerals	3
3. Numbering	5
4. Memorable Numbers	7
5. Numerically Speaking	9
6. Colorful Numerals	11
7. Your Lucky Number	13
8. Thirteen	15
Arithmetic	
9. The Cost of Candy	17
10. The Right Change	19
11. Symbols	20
12. What Is *Your* Address?	22
13. Wrong Number	23
14. Mistakes	24
15. Ethiopian Multiplication	25
16. Successive Subtraction	26
17. Three Problems	28
18. Zero	29
19. What Is the Problem?	30
20. Fill in the Circles	31
21. More than Four Ways	32
22. Two More Dollars	33
23. Tom's Game	34
24. Tasks	35

Contents

25. Sophie's Problem	37
26. Ask the Right Questions	39
27. Find the Problem	40
28. Relationships	41
29. Planning a Colorful Event	43

Measurement

30. Two Mistakes	46
31. Half as Much	47
32. Two-by-Fours	49
33. Hot and Deep	51
34. Enough	53
35. Converting	55
36. Sea Time	56
37. Mixing Bleach	58

Geometry

38. Geometric Artistry	59
39. Shapes	61
40. Concentric Squares?	62
41. Figuring	64
42. Geometric Flooring	66
43. Frames and Panes	67
44. A New Route	69
45. A Gem of an Idea	70
46. Mowing 'Em Down	71
47. Kitchen Design	72
48. Going Around	74
49. Count the Ways	78
50. What's the Angle?	80
51. Configurations	81

Ratios

52. Parts	83
53. Equal Parts	84
54. Percentage Baseball	85
55. Tracy Figures	86

56.	Sprouts	87
57.	Twice as Much	89
58.	Getting Smaller	92
59.	More Stop than Go	94
60.	"How's the Weather Up There?"	96

Algebra

61.	The Puddlejumpers and Puffers Parade	97
62.	Less than $10.00	99
63.	Multiple Distributions	100
64.	Nine Left	101

Applications

65.	Story Problems	102
66.	The Sketch	104
67.	It Figures	106
68.	Four Plus Seven Make Nine	108
69.	Mel Comes Through	109
70.	How Do You Poach a Roach?	110
71.	A Square Inch	112
72.	Calculating by Hand	114
73.	Yebas for Dollars	116
74.	Back to the Basics	118
75.	Experimenting with Humor	120
76.	Profits	122
77.	It's Easy Venn You Know How	124
78.	No Labels	126
79.	The Gopher	130
80.	Lucky You?	132
81.	Educated Guesses	134
82.	Community Fitness	136
83.	Relative Comfort	137
84.	Not Covered	140
85.	Ice Fishing	141

Notes on the Units   143

Foreword

Almost all serious scholars of creative behavior agree that attitude and skills are important in creative achievement. Throughout his long career, R. E. Myers has been a master at stimulating the development of the attitudes and skills that facilitate creative achievements. This series of *Cognitive Connections* in mathematics, science, social studies, and language arts is itself a creative achievement because in ingenious ways, it spurs young people to use their intelligences. Each of these books affords students a great deal of practice in using creative and critical thinking skills as they work in these disciplines.

In the fields of creativity testing, creative learning and teaching, and creative achievements in adult life, my associates and I have developed devices that aim to accomplish specific outcomes. We have regarded the following functions as most important in helping teachers and others do a better job:

- making teachers, psychologists, students, and parents aware of the most important creative abilities/skills that need to be developed or practiced
- making them aware of the student's strengths for creative learning and problem solving
- making them aware of gaps or deficits in the student's repertoire of creative abilities/skills
- providing a basis for generating learning activities and planning instruction
- providing a basis for generating evaluation procedures that assess not only the traditionally tested types of outcomes but also some of the more elusive objectives of education

A list of abilities or skills is given below and elaborated on in my *The Search for Satori and Creativity* and *The Incubation Model of Teaching*. The skills are all to be found in Myers's exercises in this series of books. I am sure that there are other creative abilities or skills, and some of those listed below will in time be renamed.

Finding the problem
Producing alternatives (fluency)
Being original
Being flexibl
Abstracting (highlighting the essence)
Elaborating
Keeping open (delaying closure)
Being aware of and using emotions
Putting ideas into context

Combining and synthesizing
Visualizing richly and colorfully
Fantasizing
Using movement and sound
Looking at things from a different perspective
Visualizing things internally
Extending boundaries
Using humor
Respecting infinity

I am also sure these abilities or skills will be called forth most effectively in response to the activities in this book and to the subject matter taught.

E. Paul Torrance *(April 10, 1995)*

Introduction

Although the units in this book are arranged in sections that roughly correspond to a sequence of middle-grade math skills, within each section there is a variation of complexity that provides you with a good deal of flexibility. If you teach advanced students, you can find several challenging activities in the arithmetic section. Conversely, many of the geometry units are simple enough for less advanced students. As is typical of creative thinking activities, a great number of units should challenge all students.

The chart that follows lists the creative and critical thinking skills called for in the units. You can use the chart to promote thinking skills and help your students develop those skills. Often, a skill such as originality or fluency is emphasized in books that promote creative thinking while other skills such as withholding judgment and being flexible are excluded. As important as original thinking is, the individual also needs the other creative and critical thinking skills to bring ideas to fruition.

THINKING SKILLS CHART

UNIT	Being Sensitive/Finding the Problem	Producing Alternatives	Being Flexible	Being Original	Highlighting the Essence	Elaborating	Keeping Open	Being Aware of Emotions	Putting Ideas into Context	Combining and Synthesizing	Visualizing Richly and Colorfully	Enjoying and Using Fantasy	Making It Swing, Making It Ring	Looking at It in Another Way	Visualizing Internally	Breaking Through/Extending Boundaries	Letting Humor Flow	Orienting to the Future	Analyzing	Making Judgments	Hypothesizing
1. Twos and Threes	✓																				
2. Live Numerals		✓							✓										✓	✓	
3. Numbering								✓	✓												
4. Memorable Numbers		✓						✓													
5. Numerically Speaking									✓		✓								✓	✓	
6. Colorful Numerals											✓										
7. Your Lucky Number									✓		✓								✓	✓	
8. Thirteen						✓	✓														
9. The Cost of Candy		✓																			
10. The Right Change						✓													✓	✓	
11. Symbols		✓																	✓	✓	
12. What Is Your Address?		✓							✓												
13. Wrong Number		✓				✓													✓	✓	
14. Mistakes																					
15. Ethiopian Multiplication		✓																			
16. Successive Subtraction																					
17. Three Problems		✓																			
18. Zero																					
19. What Is the Problem?		✓				✓													✓	✓	
20. Fill in the Circles						✓													✓	✓	
21. More than Four Ways							✓												✓	✓	
22. Two More Dollars	✓																				
23. Tom's Game	✓							✓											✓	✓	
24. Tasks	✓					✓													✓	✓	
25. Sophie's Problem						✓	✓												✓	✓	
26. Ask the Right Questions							✓												✓	✓	
27. Find the Problem				✓			✓												✓	✓	
28. Relationships																			✓	✓	

THINKING SKILLS CHART
(CONTINUED)

UNIT	Being Sensitive/Finding the Problem	Producing Alternatives	Being Flexible	Being Original	Highlighting the Essence	Elaborating	Keeping Open	Being Aware of Emotions	Putting Ideas into Context	Visualizing and Synthesizing	Enjoying and Using Colorfully	Making It Swing, Making It Ring	Looking at It in Another Way	Visualizing Internally	Breaking Through/Extending Boundaries	Letting Humor Flow	Orienting to the Future	Analyzing	Making Judgments	Hypothesizing
29. Planning a Colorful Event									✓									✓	✓	
30. Two Mistakes	✓																	✓		
31. Half as Much		✓	✓											✓				✓	✓	
32. Two by Fours		✓	✓															✓		
33. Hot and Deep		✓	✓	✓																
34. Enough	✓																	✓		
35. Converting		✓	✓															✓	✓	
36. Sea Time	✓							✓										✓		
37. Mixing Bleach			✓					✓										✓	✓	
38. Geometric Artistry			✓					✓	✓	✓										
39. Shapes	✓ ✓																			
40. Concentric Squares?		✓ ✓	✓																	
41. Figuring		✓ ✓	✓																	
42. Geometric Flooring			✓																	
43. Frames and Panes	✓	✓																		
44. A New Route		✓	✓															✓		
45. A Gem of an Idea	✓	✓	✓						✓											
46. Mowing 'Em Down	✓	✓	✓						✓	✓	✓							✓ ✓	✓	
47. Kitchen Design	✓	✓	✓						✓	✓								✓ ✓		
48. Going Around	✓ ✓									✓								✓ ✓	✓	
49. Count the Ways		✓																✓ ✓		
50. What's the Angle?		✓						✓												
51. Configurations								✓										✓		
52. Parts	✓	✓																✓	✓	
53. Equal Parts	✓	✓																✓		
54. Percentage Baseball			✓ ✓															✓ ✓	✓	
55. Tracy Figures																		✓	✓	
56. Sprouts										✓								✓		

THINKING SKILLS CHART
(CONTINUED)

UNIT	Being Sensitive/Finding the Problem	Producing Alternatives	Being Flexible	Being Original	Highlighting the Essence	Elaborating	Keeping Open	Being Aware of Emotions	Putting Ideas into Context	Combining and Synthesizing	Visualizing Richly and Colorfully	Enjoying and Using Fantasy	Making It Swing, Making It Ring	Looking at It in Another Way	Visualizing Internally	Breaking Through	Letting Humor Flow	Orienting to the Future	Extending Boundaries	Analyzing	Making Judgments	Hypothesizing
57. Twice as Much	✓																			✓		✓
58. Getting Smaller		✓																		✓	✓	✓
59. More Stop than Go		✓			✓											✓				✓	✓	✓
60. "How's the Weather Up There?"	✓																			✓		✓
61. The Puddlejumpers and Puffers	✓	✓																		✓		✓
62. Less than $10.00		✓																		✓		✓
63. Multiple Distributions																				✓		✓
64. Nine Left	✓																			✓		✓
65. Story Problems		✓																		✓		✓
66. The Sketch				✓							✓									✓		✓
67. It Figures	✓																			✓		✓
68. Four Plus Seven Make Nine			✓																	✓		✓
69. Mel Comes Through					✓			✓												✓		✓
70. How Do You Poach a Roach?											✓									✓		✓
71. A Square Inch											✓									✓		✓
72. Calculating by Hand		✓																		✓		✓
73. Yebas for Dollars		✓							✓											✓		✓
74. Back to the Basics																				✓		✓
75. Experimenting with Humor																	✓			✓	✓	✓
76. Profits	✓																			✓	✓	✓
77. It's Easy Venn You Know How	✓	✓					✓													✓		✓
78. No Labels						✓														✓		✓
79. The Gopher		✓																		✓	✓	✓
80. Lucky You?						✓														✓		✓
81. Educated Guesses		✓																		✓	✓	✓
82. Community Fitness								✓												✓	✓	✓
83. Relative Comfort																				✓		✓
84. Not Covered	✓																					
85. Ice Fishing																				✓		✓

To the Teacher

The Critical Importance of Attitudes

In the past twenty-five years and more a tremendous amount of writing has appeared in popular and professional publications concerning the nurturing of creativity. Whatever else has been said, or can be said, the *attitudes* that exist in any situation are the most important elements in creative production. In the classroom the individual student's attitude, the teacher's attitude, and the attitudes of the student's classmates concerning his or her ability to produce ideas are all-important. If the student has an attitude that his or her ideas are worthwhile and if the student's teacher and classmates reinforce this attitude, positive things will happen, if only to the student's sense of self-worth. Conversely, no one is more vulnerable to harsh criticism than the person who reveals his or her original ideas, for those ideas tell everyone who he or she is.

Some clear-headed critics have noted the apparent paradox in the devising of methods, systems, programs, and the like for freeing creative abilities. They point out, quite correctly, that these formulations are antithetical to the spirit of creativity. Our defense for series such as *Cognitive Connections* is that through their use students and teachers alike often discover hidden talents in students who heretofore hadn't been known to have them.

Even a contrived activity in producing novel ideas is more conducive to the development of a talent, however slight, than is an exercise in repeating or retrieving someone else's information. In a perfect world, everyone could discover his or her talents by progressing through a series of experiences that would thereby inevitably help the individual to develop those talents. Our world often seems to be designed to discourage or even snuff out the talents of too many individuals. *Cognitive Connections* is an attempt to give the student an opportunity now and then to express ideas that might otherwise not be expressed.

Preferred Ways of Learning in the Disciplines

Most educators nowadays agree that teachers are most effective in teaching thinking skills when the skills are employed naturally by students who are engaged in activities in the regular curriculum. That is why *Cognitive Connections* is comprised of activities in social studies, language arts, science, and mathematics.

It is also apparent that more thinking skills are utilized when students are allowed to use their preferred sense modalities, thus ensuring them of more successful experiences in acquiring skills, abilities, and information. The current emphasis upon the importance of appealing to the many intelligences of young people is most welcome.

For more than three decades the author, in collaboration with E. Paul Torrance, has attempted to incorporate activities that involve young people in drawing, manipulating, acting, singing, dancing, constructing, touching, and interacting with all kinds of people. *We have believed that the key to unlocking a child's potential is, and always has been, in allowing her or him to succeed.* By providing a wide range of opportunities for the young person to express himself or herself, a teacher can greatly increase the chance that she or he will succeed.

This book calls for all of Gardner's seven intelligences (Gardner 1993, Armstrong 1994) in a multimodal approach to stimulating learning. The emphasis, however, is upon the creative thinking skills described by E. Paul Torrance in *The Incubation Model of Teaching* (1990) and in his test manuals (Torrance 1979). We have attempted to encourage each of those eighteen skills in the units that follow. We have listed the thinking skills called for in *Cognitive Connections* in the previous section.

The Importance of Practice

As is the case with all skills, creative and critical thinking skills must be practiced in order for individuals to benefit from them. In the laboratory and in the classroom, there has been abundant evidence that all skills have to be developed by deliberate, direct attention. To illustrate the importance of practice, we can cite the experiences of the students of an entire school, Twin Hills Middle School of Sebastopol, California. After being among the lowest in the state in a test of basic skills, with only 35 percent of its students managing to score "proficient" or better in writing, in only two years they improved to second highest in the state in math, with 61 percent, and highest in their county in reading, with 78 percent.

After the students had scored so poorly on the statewide tests, the teachers and administrators of Twin Hills Middle School decided that the low scores were unacceptable and embarked on a program that was astoundingly successful. Students produced autobiographical essays and poems. They composed math and science reports, explained how they had analyzed statistics, created miniature history books for younger students, and penned mock letters about math data to government officials. In math classes students kept math journals to explain how they calculated their answers. Sometimes they were given an answer "Jeopardy"-style and had to write their own questions. In one project, students made paper airplanes and recorded their landing accuracy by launching them toward a wall. For their final exam, students analyzed the statistics they had gathered and wrote reports for NASA recommending certain aircraft licensing. They had to support their reports with math statistics and written explanations. Posters lined the walls of classrooms for other projects, such as the one in which students wrote mock letters to the secretary of the navy to explain results to math problems. Quite simply, the program was a success because students wrote—and therefore thought—about all of their studies.

The Role of Evaluation in Creative Thinking

You will note that critical thinking skills are listed along with the creative thinking skills in the chart giving the thinking skills called for in each unit of this book. It isn't said often enough that critical thinking is a necessary component of creative thinking. The evaluation stage of the creative process is crucial to the final production of something worthwhile. In contradistinction to some writers, however, we don't believe creative thinking is a necessary component of critical thinking, at least when the primary focus and/or motivation is to evaluate. A critical set can vitiate creative production.

As a teacher, you may often be puzzled to know how to react when a student produces a truly imaginative response to an assignment. Most of the units in this series encourage speculative responses, and so you may wonder how to evaluate them. Inasmuch as these units often require investigation and critical thinking as well, you may have a problem if you are attempting to grade your students' responses. We sympathize with you. Here are only a couple of suggestions, but we hope they will help.

It has become traditional practice for teachers to eschew premature evaluation and not try to grade creative productions in their early stages. In the case of a unit that deserves your personal interaction with a student, you can follow the procedure of the English psychologist Edward de Bono (1974). He believes you should begin an evaluation with some kind of praise for the effort of the student. Then you should ask for clarification of unclear, incorrect, or undeveloped elements. Following that phase, you can criticize—gently—those elements most in need of correction, restructuring, or deletion. The fourth and final phase consists of encouraging the student to amplify a solution, to fill in gaps, to redefine the problem, to press his or her thinking further, or to do whatever else is needed in order to obtain a satisfactory product. When you have completed this procedure, a grade—if a grade is necessary—can be given to the student's efforts.

Often a unit will have elements that can be readily assessed. Is there evidence that the student (a) understood what was being asked, (b) attempted to utilize available resources to come up with a satisfactory solution or product, and (c) went beyond the minimal requirements of giving an answer? Regardless of how accurate or realistic the response is, there should be evidence of thinking about the questions of the unit, and we hope the thinking was penetrating and far-reaching. This process will take student effort and, although it can't actually be equated with a grade, you can evaluate that effort. At the end of the book, we have provided a few comments and a solution for each unit, if a solution is called for.

Your Role as Co-Author

What we have attempted to do in this book is to give some very explicit procedures for encouraging students to think both creatively and critically. We have also provided a pedagogical framework that undergirds the units. We hope to have explained the "why" as well as the "what" and "how" of using the units. You can present these ideas for stimulating thinking at whatever occasions seem propitious. We ardently hope you will familiarize yourself with the units, noting the ones that seem likely to accomplish whatever objectives you have for your class during the year. You can use a number of units on any occasion when you think they will foster learning. Others may be used most effectively when events and circumstances make their administration timely.

We have tried to select topics that will interest your students, but, since we don't know them, we will probably miss the mark more than once. To ensure the success of those units you think may be most promising, we encourage you to modify and adapt them in your own way. It seems reasonable to us that, since you know your students' abilities and backgrounds, you can improve nearly everything in this book. We urge you to do so whenever you see the opportunity.

References

Armstrong, T. 1994. *Multiple Intelligences in the Classroom*. Alexandria, Va.: Association for Supervision and Curriculum Development.

de Bono, E. 1974. *Thinking Course for Juniors*. Dorset, United Kingdom: Direct Education Services.

Gardner, H. 1993. *Multiple Intelligences: The Theory in Practice*. New York: BasicBooks.

Torrance, E. P. 1979a. *The Search for Satori and Creativity*. Buffalo, N.Y.: Creative Education Foundation.

———. 1979b. *The Torrance Tests of Creative Thinking*. Bensenville, Ill.: Scholastic Testing Service.

Torrance, E. P., and H. T. Safter. 1990. *The Incubation Model of Teaching*. Buffalo, N.Y.: Bearly Limited.

Cognitive

Connections

Student Activities Section

Name _____

 # Twos and Threes

One day Pat gets an idea. He looks at himself in the mirror and sees a lot of pairs. He sees a pair of eyes, a pair of ears, a pair of cheeks, a pair of arms, a pair of hands, and a pair of legs. His idea is that a lot of things come in pairs. His mother had twins after he was born, and so he may be more aware of twos than other children are.

When Pat goes to his room that night, he sees more pairs. He takes off his shoes, the rest of his clothes, and his eyeglasses. He looks at a picture of himself on a bike. The bike has two wheels. Then he looks at a picture of his big brother standing beside his car. It has two front wheels and two back wheels.

"There sure are a lot of twos," Pat thinks.

There are a lot of twos in the world, all right. Are there also a lot of threes? What comes in threes? Name all of the things that come in threes that you see every day.

_____
_____
_____
_____
_____
_____
_____
_____
_____

Cognitive Connections © 1996 Zephyr Press, Tucson, Arizona

Name _____

 **Live Numerals**

If you were a numeral, which one would you like to be? 1? (You could say, "I'm Number One!") 2? 3? 4? 5? 6? 7? 8? 9? 0? _____

Why would you like to be that numeral? _____
_____
_____

Could you run better if you were that numeral? _____
Why or why not? _____
_____
_____

Could you dance better if you were that numeral? _____
Why or why not? _____
_____
_____

Could you sing better if you were that numeral? _____
Why or why not? _____
_____
_____

Could you think better if you were that numeral? _____
Why or why not? _____
_____
_____

(Continued)

Cognitive Connections © 1996 Zephyr Press, Tucson, Arizona

3

Name _____

Let's say that there are other living numerals besides you. Which one would be your best friend? _____
Why? _____
_____
_____
_____

Which ones would you have very little to do with? _____
Why? _____
_____
_____
_____

Name _____

 # Numbering

A. Here are some numerals:

1, 2, 3, 4, 5, 6, 7, 8, 9

Think about each of these numerals. What do you know about them? Write five mathematical facts about any one of them.

1. _____
2. _____
3. _____
4. _____
5. _____

B. Now think about any two of the numerals in combination. For example, if you take the first two numerals, 1 and 2, in that order, you will have 12. That is a very familiar combination of numerals, of course. The number twelve is important in keeping track of time, and it is also important in counting objects. When do we count objects by twelves?

_____
_____
_____
_____
_____
_____

(Continued)

Name _____

C. Come up with your favorite two-digit number by combining two numerals.

_____

D. Which combination of two numerals gives a number that best expresses your best friend's personality? _____

Why does it express your best friend's personality? _____

_____

_____

_____

_____

_____

Which combination of two numerals gives a number that expresses the personality of a parent or guardian? _____

Why does it represent your parent or guardian? _____

_____

_____

_____

_____

_____

Name _____

 # Memorable Numbers

A. Are you good with dates? Some people have a knack for remembering the dates of historical events or the dates of important happenings in their lives. Other people have trouble keeping track of any dates. They forget dates or get them mixed up. There are mnemonic devices for helping anyone remember dates and other numbers, but most people don't remember to use them!

One way to remember something such as a telephone number is to find relationships among the numerals. For instance, a phone number such as 345-6789 is very easy to remember because the numerals are in consecutive order. Businesses try to make certain that they have telephone numbers that are easily remembered. A great number of businesses, agencies, and associations rely upon the letters on the dial of the telephone to help people remember their numbers, and so they tell people to dial something with a word that characterizes them. (800-CRANKIT for a car battery company and 485-BIRD for the Audubon Society are examples.) Name at least three other businesses or agencies that use this technique of helping people remember their numbers. Give their telephone numbers.

1. _____

2. _____

3. _____

B. Devise a seven-digit telephone number that is easy to remember because it illustrates the operations of addition or subtraction.

_____

(Continued)

Cognitive Connections © 1996 Zephyr Press, Tucson, Arizona

C. What operations does 465-7687 represent?

D. Is it possible to have a seven-digit telephone number that represents the operations of multiplication or division?

Name _____

5 Numerically Speaking

0 1 2 3 4 5 6 7 8 9

Which of the above numerals is musical? _____

Why do you think so? _____
_____
_____

Which of the numerals is happy? _____

Why do you think so? _____
_____
_____

Which one is sad? _____

Why do you think it is sad? _____
_____
_____

Which of the numerals is pretty? _____

What makes you think so? _____
_____
_____

Which one is old? _____

Why do you think it is old? _____
_____
_____

(Continued)

Cognitive Connections © 1996 Zephyr Press, Tucson, Arizona

Name _____

Put two of the numerals together that you think belong together. _____

Why do they belong together? _____

_____

_____

What are they like when they are together? _____

_____

_____

Name _____

 # Colorful Numerals

A. If every numeral were to be a color, what color do you think 1 would be? Red? Blue? Brown? Green? Should it be green because it is the first numeral, and since we start with 1, it's a "go"?

_____
_____
_____

What color would 2 be? _____
_____
_____

B. What color would you assign to 0? Would it be white? _____ Why would you think of white for 0? _____

_____

Would it be black? _____ Why or why not? _____

_____

Is black a color? _____ Explain. _____

_____
_____

How many primary colors are there? _____

C. List your colors for the first ten numerals.

0 _____ 5 _____
1 _____ 6 _____
2 _____ 7 _____
3 _____ 8 _____
4 _____ 9 _____

(Continued)

Cognitive Connections © 1996 Zephyr Press, Tucson, Arizona

11

Name _____

D. Which should be the brightest numeral? _____ Why? _____
   _____
   _____

   Which should be the dullest? _____ Why? _____
   _____
   _____

   Look over your choices. Do you want to change any? If so, strike out your original choice and put in your new choice.

E. Would it be a good idea to give different shades to two-digit numerals? _____
   Explain. _____
   _____
   _____
   _____

Name _____

 # Your Lucky Number

A. Do you have a lucky number? _____ Is it 3? _____ Is it 7? _____

Those are many people's favorite numbers, and there are several hypotheses about why some people prefer those numbers and think the numbers are lucky. Our experiences in life are apt to make us think a certain number is luckier for us than others. For instance, an individual may think 11 is lucky because he was born on that date, or because she chose it in a game and then won. There are any number of reasons people have for regarding numbers as lucky.

B. What is the answer to these mathematical questions? _____

2 x 2 =   5 - 1 =

3 + 1 =   8 ÷ 2 =

How do you feel about the number 4? Do you have any particular feelings when you encounter 4 by itself? _____ What are they?

_____
_____

Do you have any reactions when you are assigned the number 4 in a group or in a game? _____ If so, what are they?

_____
_____
_____

Does the number 4 make you feel good?
If so, when would it make you feel good?

_____
_____
_____

Would it ever make you feel bad? _____

When would it make you feel bad? _____

_____

(Continued)

Cognitive Connections © 1996 Zephyr Press, Tucson, Arizona   13

Name _____

C. In what situation could 1 be lucky? _____
_____
_____
_____

In what situation could 1 be unlucky? _____
_____
_____
_____

In what way could 5 be lucky? _____
_____
_____
_____

In what way could 5 be unlucky? _____
_____
_____
_____

How could the number 9 be lucky? _____
_____
_____
_____

Could having a certain number make you more confident? _____
How could it make you more confident? _____
_____
_____
_____

Name _____

 # Thirteen

A. You are probably aware that some tall buildings have twelfth and fourteenth floors, but not thirteenth floors. The buildings may have only sixteen stories, but you can get off at the seventeenth floor! The reason is that the number thirteen is widely believed to be an unlucky number (although some athletes and others have deliberately chosen to be identified with it).

Human beings have many superstitions. Every group of people on Earth has superstitions. Numbers are particularly likely to be regarded as having special significance or power. Numerology is a method of explaining the events in people's lives by taking into account the number of letters in a person's name and the numbers in his or her date of birth. Numerologists base their numerological calculations on their belief that all numbers vibrate. Whether you believe that numbers have special powers or not, your behavior can be modified by such a belief.

There are several numeration systems in use by people throughout the world. The one we have, and the most commonly used, is the decimal or base 10 system. Some of the other numeration systems that can be used are the base 5 system, which uses five digits; the base 2 system, which uses two digits; and the duodecimal system, which uses 12 digits.

The base 5 system uses 0, 1, 2, 3, and 4. In this system the numeral 10 (one, zero) stands for five, the base of the system. It means "one five plus no ones." How is the number 13 in the decimal system represented in the base 5 system?

_____

If we changed to the base 5 system, replacing the decimal system that we have, would people still be superstitious about the number 13? _____

Why or why not? _____

_____

_____

_____

(Continued)

Name _____

B. Let's say your favorite—or "lucky"—number is 16. How is 16 represented in the base 5 system?

_____

Do you think you could ever shift from 16 to its counterpart in the base 5 system? _____

Why or why not? _____

_____

_____

C. What is your favorite number? _____

What is it in the base 5 system? _____

Do you think getting that number or having it assigned to you really helps? ____

Why or why not? _____

_____

_____

Do you behave differently if you are given your favorite number when individuals are assigned different numbers, as in games, lotteries, tests, and so on? Give as much evidence for your answer as possible.

_____

_____

_____

_____

_____

_____

_____

_____

_____

The Cost of Candy

How much do these things cost today?

    a candy bar? _____

    a bottle of pop? _____

    a pencil? _____

How much do you think each of those things will cost when you are a grown-up?

    a candy bar? _____

    a bottle of pop? _____

    a pencil? _____

How much more will the candy bar cost then than it does now?

How much more will the bottle of pop cost?

How much more will the pencil cost?

(Continued)

Name _____

If you have a child, will you give him or her money each week? _____

If you do, how much money will you give your child? _____

How much more or less will your child get than you get now? _____

Will the cost of everything keep going up, or will some things cost less when you are a grown-up?

_____
_____
_____

Why do you think so? _____
_____
_____
_____
_____
_____
_____
_____

Name _____

The Right Change

You walk into a convenience store and observe the end of a sale. The clerk is just giving a customer a bag and some coins, saying " . . . and sixty-five cents is your change." The customer starts to leave the store, but then she turns and looks at the coins in her hand.

"I thought the sticker on the bottle said $4.25," she says to the clerk. "You didn't give me the right change."

If the lady is correct, she should have received how much change after giving the clerk $5.00?

_____

What do you think happened?

_____
_____
_____

Is there another possibility? Don't give a hasty answer. There just might be another possibility. What is it?

_____
_____
_____

If the lady is correct and the sticker had a price of $4.25, *where* is the store?

_____
_____
_____
_____
_____
_____

Cognitive Connections © 1996 Zephyr Press, Tucson, Arizona

Name _____

 **Symbols**

A. Here are some equations:

    2 □ 2 = 4

    4 △ 2 = 2

    5 ○ 1 = 4

    8 □ 1 = 8

    5 ◇ 5 = 10

    9 ○ 2 = 7

    10 △ 10 = 1

Determine the sign for the symbols △, ○, □, ◇.

  △ means _____

  ○ means _____

  □ means _____

  ◇ means _____

You should have no difficulty in discovering what operations are indicated by the symbols. As a matter of fact, those shapes could be used for ÷, −, x, and + if mathematicians had so chosen hundreds of years ago.

B. Symbols are used in a great variety of ways in almost every human activity. How would you use symbols in a treasure hunt? Draw the symbols and tell how they would be used.

(Continued)

Cognitive Connections © 1996 Zephyr Press, Tucson, Arizona

Name _____

Name _____

 **What Is *Your* Address?**

A. Do you live in a magical place? Christine lives in a magical place, and so does Carla. Christine's address is 3417 Canoga Place. You can see that the number is magical because 34 is twice as much as 17. That means that the people at 3417 Canoga Place are twice as lucky as other folks. They have twice as many spiders as their neighbors. They have twice as many toothpicks and twice as many heads of lettuce as anybody in town. They probably have twice as many cats, and twice as many mice also (since the mice are tame).

Christine's grandparents are lucky, too. They live at 1357 Meadow Court. What is so wonderful about their address? Do you consider it odd?

_____

_____

If they were to move to a bigger town, they might have a bigger house number. What could that house number be if it were one digit longer? _____

Carla's address is 4408 Philbrook Lane. As you can see, that address is most magical because 4 from 4 is 0, and 4 and 4 are 8. Everyone in Carla's house is very special. They have magical elbows and magical eyelashes. They also have magical dishcloths and paper clips. Carla's family is just as lucky as Christine's family.

B. Maybe you live in a magical place. What is your address?

_____

Can you see why it is magical? If you don't have a magical address, maybe a friend has one. Explain why your address—or your friend's address—is magical. Then describe all of the magical things about where you live and the people with whom you live (or where your friend lives and the people in that place).

_____

_____

13 Wrong Number

A. Following are three groups of addition facts. In each group, one of the sums is incorrect. In the blank spaces, write the letters that are next to the wrong addition facts.

    1. (a) 5 + 8 = 13   (b) 9 + 4 = 13   (c) 7 + 8 = 14   _____

    2. (a) 3 + 5 = 9   (b) 6 + 7 = 13   (c) 9 + 5 = 14   _____

    3. (a) 8 + 8 = 16   (b) 3 + 8 = 11   (c) 7 + 9 = 15   _____

B. Now, you make up a similar exercise. Put one wrong sum in each group of three addition facts. Use addition facts that classmates often get confused about. (Make sure your other sums are right!)

14 Mistakes

A. Here are three groups of multiplication facts. In each group, one of the products is incorrect. In the blank spaces, write the letters that are next to the wrong multiplication facts.

   1. (a) 5 x 5 = 25   (b) 6 x 4 = 24   (c) 7 x 9 = 64   (d) 6 x 8 = 48   ____

   2. (a) 7 x 7 = 49   (b) 9 x 9 = 81   (c) 8 x 8 = 64   (d) 9 x 8 = 74   ____

   3. (a) 6 x 9 = 54   (b) 5 x 9 = 45   (c) 7 x 8 = 54   (d) 9 x 4 = 36   ____

B. Now, you make up a similar exercise. Put one incorrect product in each group of four multiplication facts. Use multiplication facts that people often get confused about. (Make sure your other products are right!)

15 Ethiopian Multiplication

The story goes that the people in certain Ethiopian tribes do not know how to multiply, but they can add, halve, and double numbers. Accordingly, if a shepherd is selling his sheep for $19 a head and he sells fourteen of them, he knows how much will be due him. Following is how he calculates the product:

19	x	14
9		28
4		56
2		112
1		224

He just keeps on halving the numbers in the left column until he gets to 1. He doubles the numbers in the right column until the number in the left column is 1. When he halves 19, he doesn't bother to write down 9 1/2; he just makes it 9. Similarly, when he halves 9, he rounds off the 4 1/2 to 4. Since the people of these tribes abhor even numbers, the shepherd then throws out all the even numbers on the left, as well as their "partners" on the right, so the calculations look like the following:

19	x	14		19
9		28		x 14
~~4~~		~~56~~		76
~~2~~		~~112~~		190
1		224		266
		266		

If we multiply 19 by 14, we also get 266. How do you explain how the Ethiopian shepherd got the right answer? Would it work if the 14 were on the left and the 19 were on the right? Try it.

16 Successive Subtraction

A. Division can be thought of as "successive subtraction." That is, if you have a quantity such as

· · ·

· · ·

· · ·

· · ·

(represented by the numeral 12), you can divide it in several ways by taking the same number from it more than once. If you want to divide 12 by 6, for example, you can take away 6, leaving 6, and then take away 6 again. The second operation would take everything away, leaving nothing. The operation is shown in the following way:

$$\begin{array}{r} 6\overline{)12} \\ -6 \\ \hline 6 \\ -6 \\ \hline 0 \end{array}$$

So you have taken 6 from 12 twice, and that is represented as 12 ÷ 6 = 2.

Use the same successive subtraction operation to divide 12 by 3.

(Continued)

B. Young children use this method quite often. Explain how successive subtraction works for children in the first grade who want to divide twelve cookies among three children but don't know how to divide numbers as you do.

C. Think of a situation in which using the successive subtraction method would help you if you were camping.

Name _____

17 Three Problems

If you have five marbles and you give away five, how many marbles do you have left? _____

What if you don't have any gum to chew one day? You ask your friend to give you a stick of gum. Your friend tells you no, he wants to chew all of his gum later. How many sticks of gum do you have? _____

Your mother tells you that she will give you a nickel for every weed you pull in the garden. On Monday, you don't pull any weeds. You don't pull any weeds on Tuesday or Wednesday, either. How much money do you have from pulling weeds?
_____

What is the number that is found in each of the three problems? _____

Make up a problem that has that same number in it.
_____
_____
_____
_____
_____
_____

Cognitive Connections © 1996 Zephyr Press, Tucson, Arizona

18) Zero

One of the easiest ideas in mathematics to understand is that, when zero is added to a number, the sum is the same as the number. Zero is called the "identity element" in addition. Intuitively we know that if we add zero—nothing—to something, that something is unchanged. There are all sorts of occasions in life when we see this idea in operation. If a beggar who has $5.00 asks for money and we give him nothing, he will have a total of $5.00. If Joe goes to the store to buy another bubble gum card but discovers that he has no money for the purchase, he'll still have the same number of cards in his collection when he returns home empty-handed.

WHAT'S ANOTHER BUBBLEGUM CARD? I ALREADY HAVE 2097 IN MY COLLECTION— RIGHT, SLURP?

PLUS 2097 WADS OF GUM STUCK ON YOUR BEDPOSTS!

Take the principle described above and apply it to an athletic event. Tell exactly how the principle of adding zero applies in the game, giving the particulars of the game and the contestants.

Name _____

19 What Is the Problem?

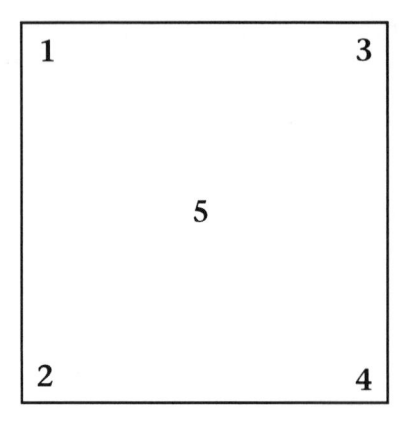

```
┌─────────────┐
│ 1         3 │
│             │
│      5      │
│             │
│ 2         4 │
└─────────────┘
```

Look at the numbers in the square. Why are they where they are? Look at them carefully. What is the problem that made someone put the numbers where they are?

_____
_____
_____

See if you can make up a problem like the one above. Fill in the numbers for the square for your problem.

_____
_____
_____

```
┌─────────────┐
│             │
│             │
│             │
│             │
│             │
└─────────────┘
```

30   Cognitive Connections © 1996 Zephyr Press, Tucson, Arizona

Name _____

20 Fill in the Circles

Here are nine circles. Arrange the counting numbers one through nine in the circles so that each connected straight line of three numbers adds up to eighteen.

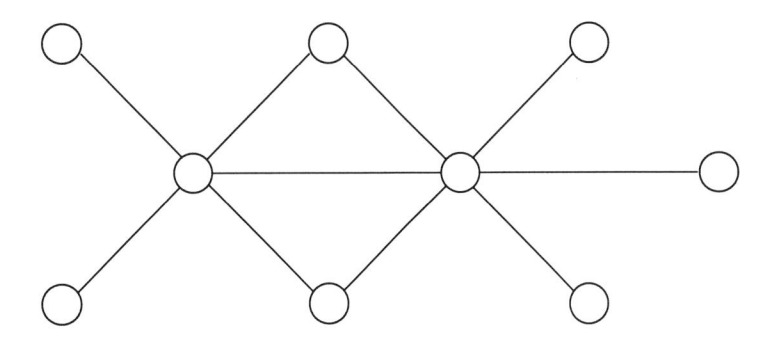

Is there only one solution to this problem? _____

Name _____

21 More than Four Ways

How many ways can five get to be fifteen? Show each one. (There are more than four ways).

How many ways can three get to be twelve? Show each way. (There are more than four ways.)

How many tens are there in an hour? _____

How many tens are in a bag of peanuts? _____

How many fives are in an ice cream cone? _____

How many twos are there in a boy's big smile? _____

22 Two More Dollars

Norma has always wanted a bike with long handlebars. She saves all of her money and needs only twenty dollars more to buy the bike. Then, on her birthday, she gets quite a few gifts. Some of her gifts are from aunts and uncles. Two uncles each give Norma five dollars. An aunt gives her two dollars.

Norma thinks, "If I get two baby-sitting jobs, I'll have enough money for the bike." Will she? Norma earns three dollars each time she sits for the Luna family.

Besides baby-sitting, Norma spends a lot of her spare time reading. She is in the sixth grade, and her teacher is having a contest to see who can read the most books. The ones who read fifty books by the time school is out in June will get a dictionary. There is a chart on the wall of the classroom. It shows Norma has read forty-two books.

Two weeks are left before vacation. Norma tells her mother, "If I read three books this week and three next week, I'll win a dictionary. But I wish Mrs. Terry had a contest for math and had a bike as a prize. I'd be sure to win."

What arithmetic fact does Norma have to learn? _____

What will happen when Norma reads six more books and tries to claim the dictionary?

Cognitive Connections © 1996 Zephyr Press, Tucson, Arizona

23 Tom's Game

Tom goes to the playground to play. He sees that there is a problem on the playground. The children aren't getting along. Some boys are playing basketball and arguing. There are three boys on each team in the game. Some girls and boys are playing Four Square. While four are playing, seven have to wait for a turn. They keep telling the ones who are playing not to be so slow.

Tom has an idea. Why not get all the boys and girls into one game? Is there a game that all of the children could play together? What is it?

Put your ideas in the space below.

Name _____

24 Tasks

Morris is an impatient young man. He likes to get things done in a hurry. Morris doesn't like to waste time. He also is quite smart. In fact, Morris is one of the smartest students in his class, Mrs. Newton's fourth grade in Washington School.

One day Mrs. Newton tells her students that when they finish a page of math problems (no words, just numbers), they may go ahead and work on the mural the class is painting. All of the answers have to be correct, though. Since Morris loves art more than he loves math, he rushes through the problems, turns in his work, and goes to the mural to paint more of his section.

After five minutes, Mrs. Newton comes up to Morris and tells him that he'll have to do two problems over—the answers are incorrect. Morris is disturbed at being interrupted and also irritated that the teacher has said he's made two mistakes.

John Henderson is a salesman in a department store. He sells men's clothing, and he gets along quite well with his customers. John is also responsible for putting money into the cash drawer every morning. A bookkeeper gives him $200 in bills and coins when John starts to work at 8:30. John has to count the money, writing down the amount in each denomination (ten-dollar bills, twenty-dollar bills, five-dollar bills, and one-dollar bills) and the amount in the different coins. Then he has to add everything up. John dislikes this part of his job, but he knows he has to do it. Occasionally the bookkeeper gives him too much or too little money.

(Continued)

Name _____

One morning John is a little late to work, so he quickly counts the amounts and rapidly adds them up. The total he comes up with is $200, so he hastily takes the money and puts it into the cash drawer. At the day's end, when he turns in the day's receipts to the bookkeeper, she counts the sales and the money and tells John he is $5.00 short.

What do Morris and John have in common? _____

_____

_____

_____

_____

What one suggestion can you give to both of them? _____

_____

_____

_____

_____

Name _____

25 Sophie's Problem

A. Mr. Jenkins, a fifth-grade teacher in a small elementary school, engages in the practice of having his students check the answers to their math problems against those in the backs of their books. He doesn't correct their answers, but they report their scores to him. One day Sophie compares her answers to those in the book and finds she has all of them right except one. Since Sophie is a whiz in math, she is a little startled to find she has missed the problem. Sophie asks Ruth if she has the answer right, and Ruth says she missed it, too. They both have the same answer, $34. The book's answer is $24.

WRONG ANSWER AGAIN! MATH CAN BE SO STUBBORN!

JUST LIKE BOYS!

Do you think that the girls' answers could be correct? _____

_____

B. Sophie decides to ask Mr. Jenkins about the problem. When he glances at her work, he says that she seems to have proceeded in the correct way. Mr. Jenkins isn't quite sure what to say to Sophie, except that she might do the problem again.

Do you think Mr. Jenkins should ask Sophie to do the problem again? _____

_____

(Continued)

Cognitive Connections © 1996 Zephyr Press, Tucson, Arizona

37

Sophie goes back to her desk and works the problem again. She still comes up with $34 as an answer.

Do you think Sophie is making the same mistake when she reworks the problem?

_____

_____

C. Here is the problem. Do it yourself and decide whether Sophie is correct.

Mr. Brown went shopping. He had $250 with him, and he went to a furniture store that took only cash. He found a small table he liked, which cost $145. Then he found a rug that would look just right in his den. It was $95. When he went to pay for his purchases, he was told that all items were 10 percent off on that day. Mr. Brown lives in a state where there is no sales tax. How much change did he receive when he handed the cashier two hundred-dollar bills and a fifty-dollar bill?

Name _____

26 Ask the Right Questions

We all solve problems every day of our lives, whether we are aware of doing so or not. But we are not always effective in solving our problems. We can be more successful if we learn the elements of solving problems and then learn how to tackle problems.

Problems have two main parts, the questions and the facts. First, you must understand the question that is being asked. Second, you must look for the facts or information that you need to answer the question. You can become a better problem solver by learning to ask appropriate questions. Write a question that can be answered by analyzing the following information.

1. A hummingbird egg weighs 0.6 gram. A chicken egg weighs 75.0 grams.
Question: _____
_____

2. In twelve hours you blink your eyes about 7,200 times.
Question: _____
_____

3. A queen bee can lay about 2,200 eggs in one day.
Question: _____
_____

4. A hot dog costs 90¢ and a soft drink costs 50¢ at the games.
Question: _____
_____

5. A movie costs $4.00 for adults and $2.00 for children under 16.
Question: _____
_____

6. Bob is 180 centimeters tall and Michael is 168 centimeters tall.
Question: _____
_____

7. Ewes weigh from 100 pounds to 225 pounds when they are adults; rams weigh from 150 to 350 pounds when grown.
Question: _____
_____

Cognitive Connections © 1996 Zephyr Press, Tucson, Arizona

27 Find the Problem

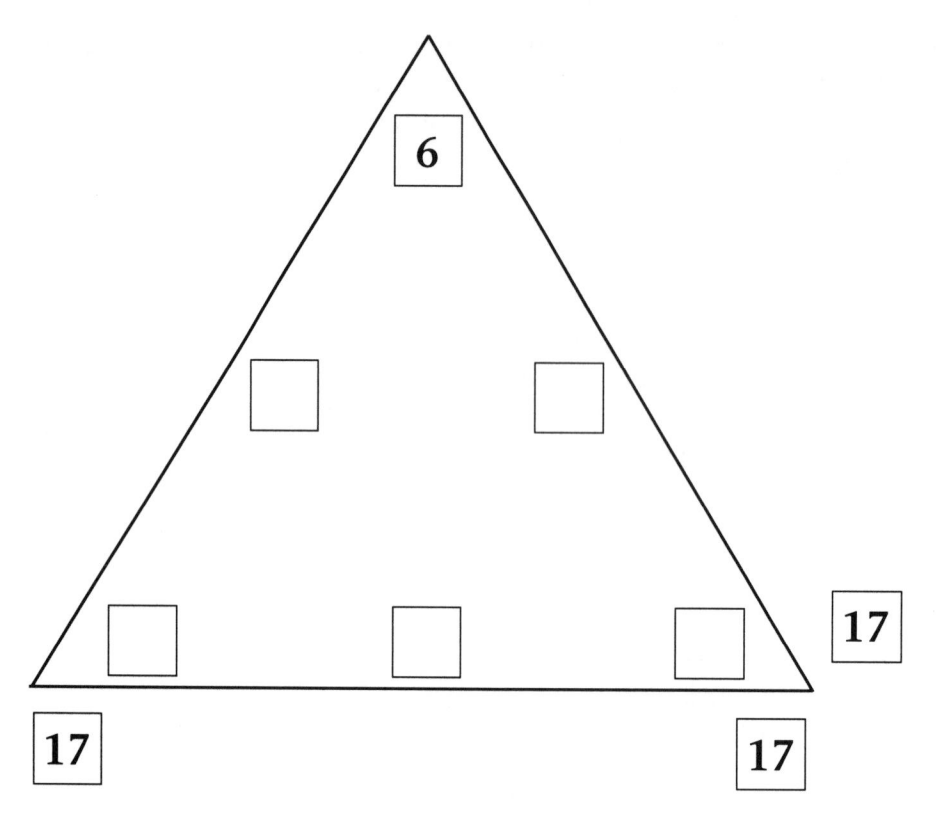

[6]

[17]

[17] [17]

Here are some squares inside and outside a triangle. Some contain numbers. Look at the numbers carefully. Why are they arranged in this way? What is the problem that is solved by putting additional numbers in the empty squares? When you figure out what the problem is, solve it.

28 Relationships

A. Relationships are everything in families and in arithmetic. How quarts relate to gallons, tens relate to thousands, and radii relate to circles is critical and fundamental. Although you probably haven't been required to do forty multiplication problems or thirty division problems lately, chances are that arithmetic comes into your life just about every day—and often many times a day. You may not think about arithmetic as science or art or process, but you bump up against it often. Here is a set of questions concerning arithmetic for you to think about. Give them some serious thought.

In what way is addition related to multiplication? Give a demonstration of your reasoning.

In what way is multiplication related to division? Give a demonstration of your reasoning.

In what way is division related to subtraction? Give a demonstration of your reasoning.

(Continued)

Name _____

In what way is subtraction related to addition? Give a demonstration of your reasoning.

B. After showing all of those relationships, do you believe that the basis for all arithmetic operations is addition? _____ Why or why not?

_____
_____
_____
_____
_____
_____
_____

C. Is counting the basis for all of mathematics? _____ Why or why not?

_____
_____
_____
_____
_____
_____
_____

29 Planning a Colorful Event

A. Let's imagine that you are planning a birthday party for a friend and that you are going to have it at your place. Decide how much you can spend for this imaginary party. Write the figure down here: _____

  1. What will you get for refreshments? Take a portion of the total amount you want to spend and assign it to refreshments. (You might choose to spend one-third or one-quarter for refreshments.) List what you will get and find out how much each item will cost for the number of people invited to your party. How much do you want to spend for refreshments? _____

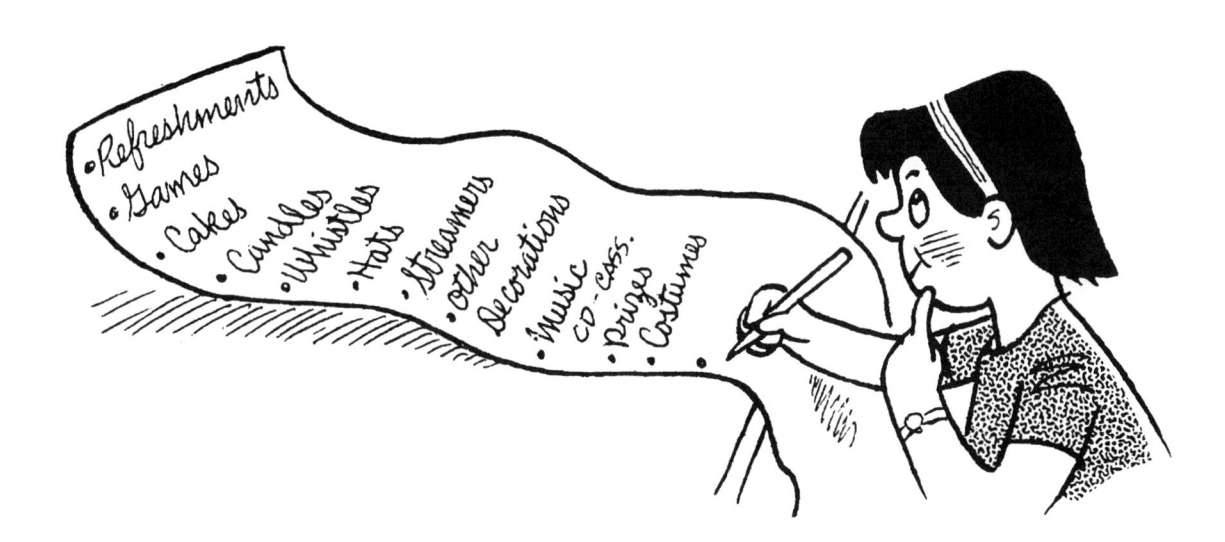

  2. If you decide to give little gifts to the guests, what will you get for favors? List what you will get and decide what portion of the total the favors will cost. (You might choose to spend from one-quarter to one-eighth for favors.) How much do you want to spend for favors? _____

(Continued)

Name _____

3. How will you decorate your place for the party? Decide upon a colorful theme and then list each of the materials you will need. Decide what portion of the total the materials will cost. (You might choose to spend from one-quarter to one-third of your budget for decorations.) How much do you want to spend for decorations? _____

4. What activities or games will your guests play at the party? List them. If any of them cost money, find out how much you will have to spend. In all, how much do you plan to spend for activities? _____

(Continued)

Name _____

B. Now look over your list. Do you have all of the things you want to have on it? If you assigned a fraction ($\frac{1}{2}$, $\frac{1}{4}$, $\frac{1}{3}$, and so on) to the categories, just make sure you don't come up with more than a whole. That is, you can't have $\frac{1}{3}$ for refreshments, $\frac{1}{4}$ for favors, and $\frac{1}{2}$ for decorations. Why not?

_____

_____

_____

Next, add up the amounts for each category, and then add those sums together to see if you are within your budgeted amount of money.

refreshments	$	_____
favors		_____
decorations		_____
activities		_____
Total	$	_____

If you find that you are over your budget, there may be a few items you can omit—or you might obtain some items without spending any money at all. Which items might you get without spending money? In case you don't want to omit any item and can't obtain anything without spending money, you may have to revise the amount you will spend. (One often has to revise a budget, as you probably know!)

30 Two Mistakes

Bill's father tells him to go up in the attic to see if he can locate the hole in the roof that has made a big wet spot in the ceiling of the living room. He also wants Bill to find out how big the hole is so that they can patch it with the proper materials.

"That leak must be something," Bill thinks, "because the wet spot got big in a hurry. I wish it would stop raining."

As soon as he enters the attic, Bill realizes that he has made a mistake. He's forgotten to bring a flashlight. Lack of light doesn't pose too much of a problem in finding the leak, however, because it is afternoon and he can see daylight in one section of the roof. Bill can see that the wind must have blown off a shingle.

Just as Bill realizes he has made another mistake, his dad yells for him to hurry up because the water is now dripping onto the floor of the living room. The second mistake is that Bill hasn't brought a tape measure or yardstick to measure the hole. He feels foolish.

His father yells again, so Bill doesn't want to go downstairs and get a yardstick or tape measure. Then it occurs to him that he can still measure the opening. What does Bill think he can use to measure the hole? Here's a clue: Bill doesn't use anything in the attic when he measures the hole.

Name _____

③① Half as Much

The Earth is becoming increasingly populated with people. It is certain that there will be less space in all of the living and working areas of cities in the future. As a result of this crowding, cities in which people now have enough elbow room will be forced to plan for more cramped working areas. Individuals and families, too, will have to learn to occupy less space.

If you have a room of your own, or if you share a room, indicate its dimensions in a floor plan sketch. Show the approximate dimensions and total square footage. (If you don't know the dimensions of your room, get a tape measure when you go home and measure them.)

Next, indicate in your drawing where the major pieces of furniture are placed in your room and where you store your clothing and other belongings.

(Continued)

Cognitive Connections © 1996 Zephyr Press, Tucson, Arizona

Name _____

Now draw the outline of your room again, but make it half as big. Then decide where your furniture and clothing and other belongings will be placed and stored. Indicate the places in your second drawing.

Name _____

32 Two by Fours

A. If you look around the place in which you live and do some careful inspecting, you'll discover that many things come in pairs. Salt and pepper shakers and pillows on a double bed are found in pairs, for example. Look a little more and you'll find that there are other things that have four parts; chairs, sofas, and tables usually have four legs. Speakers for stereo sets have two or four speakers.

It used to be that much of a house was constructed with 2-by-4-inch boards, but the dimensions of lumber sold nowadays are actually smaller. What are the real dimensions of a board sold as a two-by-four at the lumber yard?

_____

What had to happen before the smaller two-by-fours could be sold to the public?

_____
_____
_____

Do you think that the size of a two-by-four will be further reduced in the future? _____ Why or why not? Ask someone—a carpenter or builder—what the reasons are for further reducing or not reducing the two-by-four.

_____
_____
_____

B. Examine one room in your home and count the number of things that come in pairs or have two parts to them.

Number of 2s = _____

Now examine the same room and find out how many things have four parts or come in fours.

Number of 4s = _____

(Continued)

Cognitive Connections © 1996 Zephyr Press, Tucson, Arizona

Name _____

C. Why don't you design a piece of furniture, such as a chair, that has five legs? You can use the space below for your sketch.

Name _____

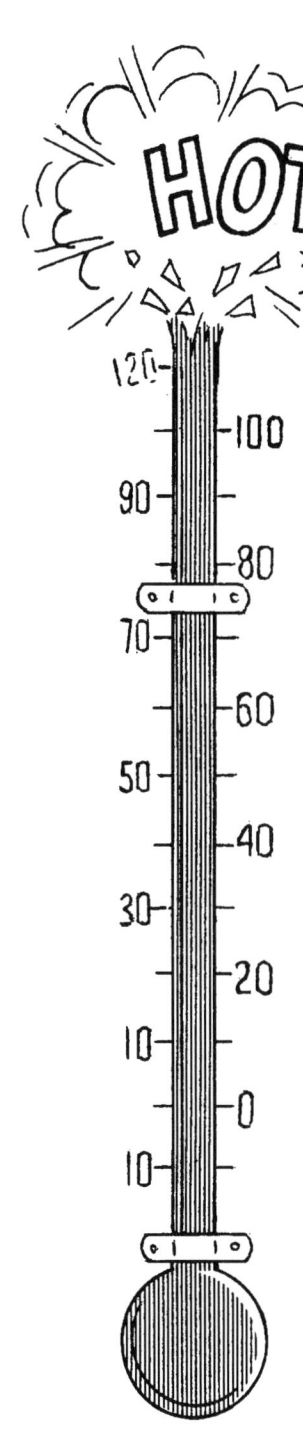

33 Hot and Deep

A. Fred is preparing a report about northern Africa. He reads that on September 13, 1922, a temperature of 136.4° Fahrenheit was recorded in Libya. What is that temperature converted to Celsius?

_____

When Mindy was aboard a sailboat last summer, she was told that the greatest depth of the harbor where they were sailing was five fathoms. How deep was the water in feet?

_____

What do these two problems have in common?

_____
_____
_____

B. Make up a third problem that can only be solved in the same way that you solved the two above.

(Continued)

Cognitive Connections © 1996 Zephyr Press, Tucson, Arizona   51

Name _____

C. Make up the same kind of problem, but solve it in a different way.

34 Enough

A. In life we have to know what is enough. We have to know when we've had a sufficient amount of nearly everything—food, drink, conversation, entertainment, exercise, and even sleep. We quantify "enough" more often than you may realize, specifying certain amounts of calories for a meal, temperatures for hot and cold, number of days rehearsing a play, and so on.

"Is it hot enough for you?" is a familiar question during summer. If someone replied to the query with: "No, it should be about 2° hotter," the person who asked the question would probably be dumbfounded. Yet the television stations and the newspapers remark about record high temperatures, and we can suppose that those days are hot enough for almost everyone, except perhaps merchants selling electric fans and air conditioners.

This exercise is an opportunity for you to do a little practical research. Why don't you find out the following:

1. The temperature at which something for dinner will be cooking at home tonight. What is recommended in the cookbook? What, if any, is the difference between the temperature of the dish cooking in your home and the recommended temperature in the cookbook?

   Name of dish _____

   Temperature at which it is cooking _____

   Temperature in the cookbook _____

   Difference _____

(Continued)

Cognitive Connections © 1996 Zephyr Press, Tucson, Arizona   53

Name _____

2. The marks on your last spelling and math tests. How many points were you above or below the passing marks?

   Score on math test _____   Passing score _____   Difference _____

   Score on spelling test _____   Passing score _____   Difference _____

3. The amount of sleep you had last night. Find out what the recommended amount is for someone your age. Then determine if you were above or below what is considered enough sleep.

   Amount of sleep last night _____

   Recommended amount of sleep _____

   Difference _____

4. The number of hours you watched television last night. If you check into one of the many articles written in newspapers and magazines about television viewing for children, you can learn what the average watching time is for someone about your age.

   Hours watching television last night _____

   Average number of hours for young people your age _____

   Difference _____

   How much television is "enough" in your opinion? _____

   How much is "enough" in your parents' opinion? _____

B. Do you see a problem in any of your findings? _____ If so, what is it?

   _____

   Should you do anything about it? If so, what should you do?

   _____
   _____
   _____
   _____
   _____

Name _____

35 Converting

A. If your friend asks you for exactly a liter of water and you have only a half-gallon jug available, what would you do to give her the liter of water?

_____
_____
_____
_____
_____

B. You remember a ruler you saw that had centimeters on one side and inches on the other. Maybe you can do something with the unmarked half-gallon jug so that you can get dual readings when it is filled with liquid. Show how it can be done with the marks for both kinds of measures. How will you distinguish between major and minor divisions?

_____
_____
_____
_____
_____
_____

Are English and metric measurements made in a similar way on other instruments? What are they?

_____
_____
_____

Cognitive Connections © 1996 Zephyr Press, Tucson, Arizona

Name _____

36 Sea Time

A. Grandfather clocks and ship's bells tell the time when people can't see clocks. A grandfather clock will chime up to twelve times to let us know the hour of the day or night, but time aboard ships is reckoned differently. There are twelve hours on the faces of clocks, but time is kept on a 24-hour basis aboard a ship. That is, time is reckoned from 0001-2400 (one minute after midnight until midnight).

Another difference is that the chimes of a grandfather clock announce the hour, whereas a bell is struck on a ship to let sailors know what time it is. When a sailor hears the bell being struck five times aboard ship, he knows it may not be the same time as when he is home hearing a grandfather clock chime five times.

Do you think sailors, in their sleep, ever get confused when they are ashore and hear a grandfather clock chiming in the middle of the night?

_____
_____
_____
_____

Does the time mechanism aboard a ship, called a chronometer, have numerals going up to 24 instead of 12?

_____
_____
_____
_____
_____
_____
_____

(Continued)

56   Cognitive Connections © 1996 Zephyr Press, Tucson, Arizona

Name _____

B. Let's presume that you are unaware of the established system for striking bells aboard a ship. Knowing nothing about that system, what is your guess as to the meaning of one bell being struck?

_____
_____
_____

What would you suppose the striking of two bells could mean?

_____
_____
_____

Devise a schedule for the striking of a bell on board a ship to let people know what time it is.

_____
_____
_____
_____
_____
_____
_____
_____

Cognitive Connections © 1996 Zephyr Press, Tucson, Arizona

37 Mixing Bleach

Let's say that you want to mix bleach and water in order to clean some outdoor furniture. You want a ratio of a quart of bleach to a gallon and a half of water. Aside from the almost-full gallon container of bleach, you have only two measuring cups and an empty clear gallon container to work with.

If you pour a quart of bleach into the gallon container and then fill it with water, there will be too high a concentration of bleach. How can you get the right mixture of water and bleach for your job?

Now suppose that just after you figure out how to get the right mixture of bleach and water, your mother comes along and tells you she has to use the two cups. Since you want to finish the job as soon as you can, you try to think how you might get the right mixture and do the job without the two measuring cups. It is possible, using only the container of bleach and the empty gallon container. How can you do it?

_____
_____
_____
_____
_____
_____

Name _____

38 Geometric Artistry

Artists who make collages with bits of paper, cloth, sand, and other such materials sometimes use geometric shapes in their work. The Cubists, a group of European artists who lived in the early 1900s, also used geometric shapes as the basis of their paintings.

Pictures made from arranging geometric shapes can be both amusing and challenging. The shapes can be put next to one another, or they can overlap. You can add straight lines to a group of shapes and come up with an interesting picture. Why don't you try to compose a geometric drawing or collage with these shapes?

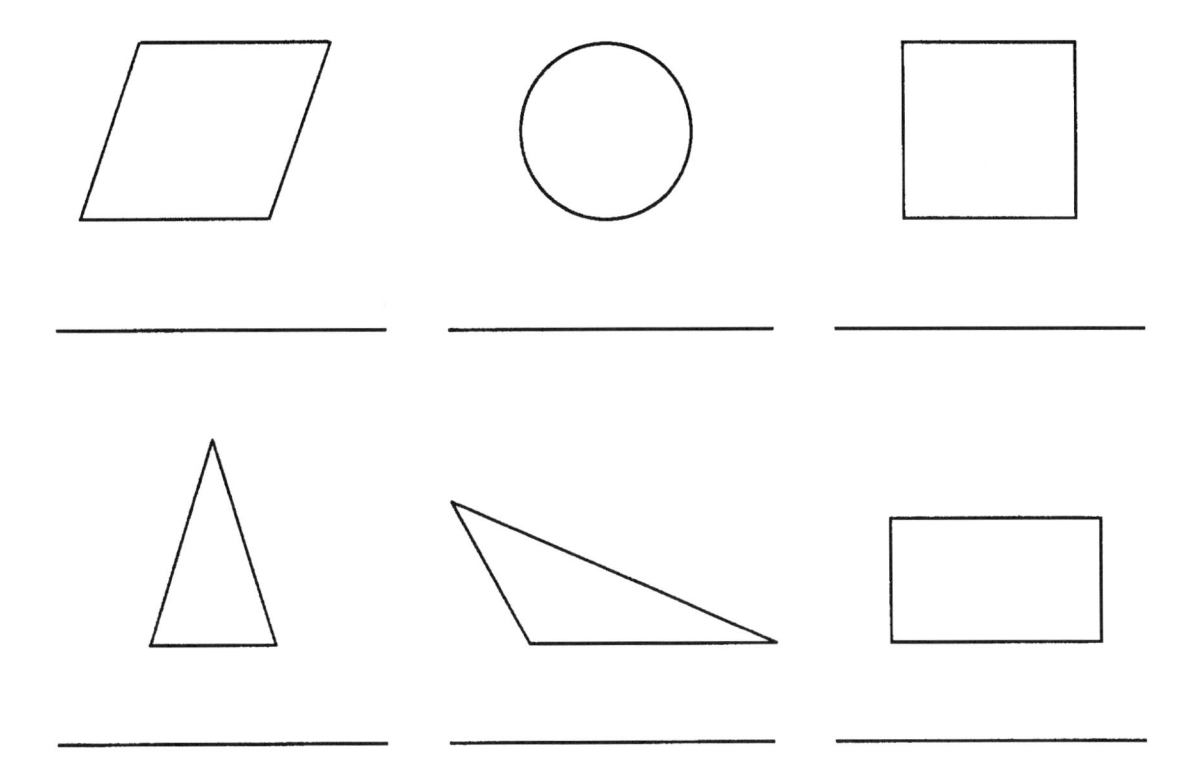

First, name each shape, distinguishing among the different triangles and rectangles.

(Continued)

Cognitive Connections © 1996 Zephyr Press, Tucson, Arizona   59

Name _____

You can use as many shapes as you wish in your creation. Use sketches to work out your ideas in the space below.

Name _____

39 Shapes

There are many, many shapes all around us. When we look at a plate, we see a circle. When we look at a desk, we see a rectangle. When we look at a sail, we see a triangle. The shape of something has a lot to do with how we use it. We need all kinds of shapes.

What shapes do we need when we write? Draw three or more and name them.

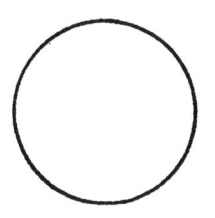

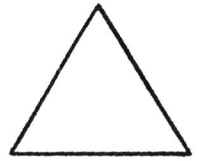

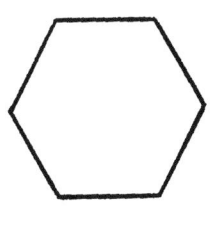

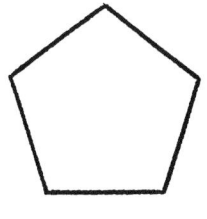

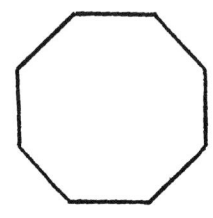

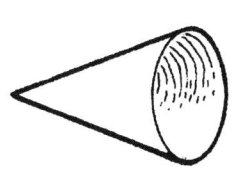

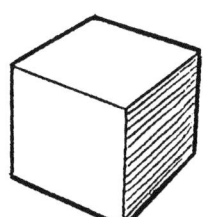

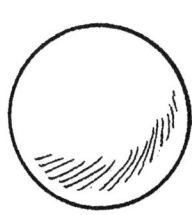

Cognitive Connections © 1996 Zephyr Press, Tucson, Arizona

Name _____

40 Concentric Squares?

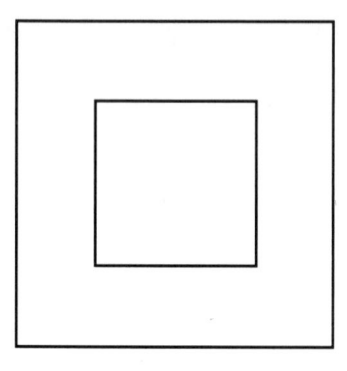

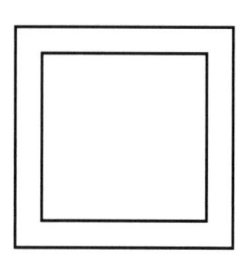

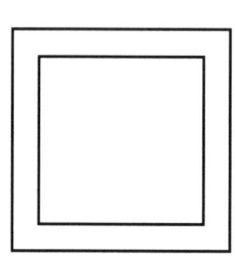

A. Examine the figures above very carefully. Is there some way that you can express a set of relationships among them? Your expression can be in any form you think is appropriate.

How else might the relationships of the figures be expressed?

(Continued)

62   Cognitive Connections © 1996 Zephyr Press, Tucson, Arizona

Name _____

What is one more way to express the relationships?

B. What is your opinion of the title of this exercise?
_____
_____

Did you measure the figures? _____ Why or why not?
_____
_____

Are the figures interesting to you in any way? _____ Explain.
_____
_____

Would you like to do anything with them? _____ If so, what would you like to do with the four figures?
_____
_____

As long as it is reasonable, go ahead!

Name _____

41 Figuring

A. When you were younger, did you ever try to find the hidden pictures in a drawing? You were supposed to make out the raccoon, bird house, rat, car, and snake that were embedded in the overall scene. Most young people enjoy that activity because it makes them really use their eyes and brains. You can play a similar game with geometric figures. Shown below are two geometric figures that will also test your eyes and brains.

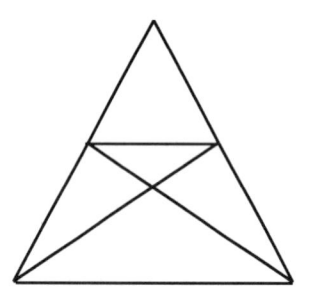

How many triangles can you find in the figure? (Hint: there are more than six.)

There are _____ triangles.

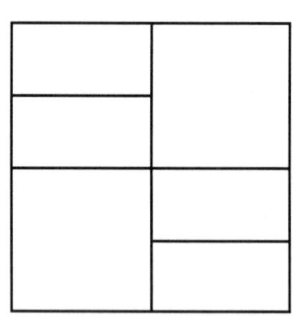

How many rectangles can you find in this figure? Remember: A square is a special kind of rectangle. (Hint: There are between twelve and eighteen.)

There are _____ rectangles.

(Continued)

64   Cognitive Connections © 1996 Zephyr Press, Tucson, Arizona

B. Ask a friend to count all of the triangles and rectangles he or she can find in the two figures. Does your friend get the same numbers as you? _____
If not, what are the differences?

_____

_____

_____

Ask another friend to count the triangles and rectangles in the two figures. Does your second friend come closer to your count or your friend's, or do all of you agree?

_____

_____

_____

C. What is the average number of triangles counted? _____

What is the average number of rectangles counted? _____

Can you come to any definite decision about how many triangles and rectangles can be found in the two figures? What do you think are the correct numbers?

_____

_____

_____

_____

42 Geometric Flooring

A. Here is a tile pattern found on the floor of a mall.

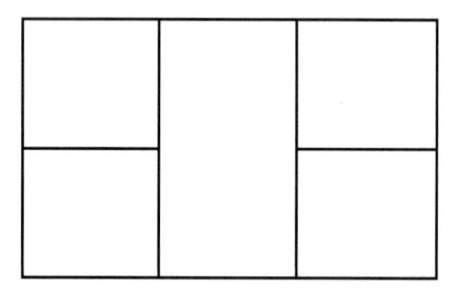

If you ignore some lines and include others, how many rectangles are there in the pattern? (Hint: Remember that a square is a rectangle.) There are more than six rectangles.

How many squares can you find? _____

B. Here is a pattern that features triangles and squares.

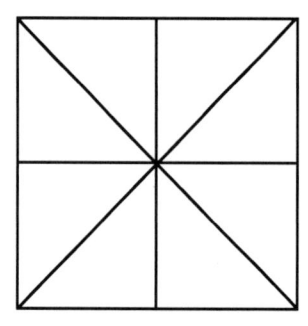

How many triangles and squares can you find by ignoring some lines and including others? (Hint: There are more than eight triangles and more than four squares.)

Triangles = _____

Squares = _____

How many isosceles triangles are there? _____

How many rectangles are there? _____

Name _____

43 Frames and Panes

Let's imagine you are planning to build a house and are drawing the windows.

Draw a window frame. Give it six panes by drawing three lines.

Draw another window frame. Is there another way to make six panes by drawing three lines? Try it.

Draw another frame. Find still another way to make six panes with three lines.

(Continued)

Cognitive Connections © 1996 Zephyr Press, Tucson, Arizona

Name _____

Draw another frame. See how many panes you get by drawing only two lines. Draw the frame another way.

Draw another frame. What is the fewest number of lines that will give you twelve panes?

Draw a triangular window. Can you make nine window panes by drawing six lines on this frame?

What kind of window would you have in your house?

Name _____

44   A New Route

Norm lives on the edge of town and raises chickens; since he has quite a few, he has extra eggs to sell to people in his neighborhood. He delivers his eggs on Mondays and Fridays before going to school in the morning. Norm has seven customers. Here are their locations on three streets near Norm's house.

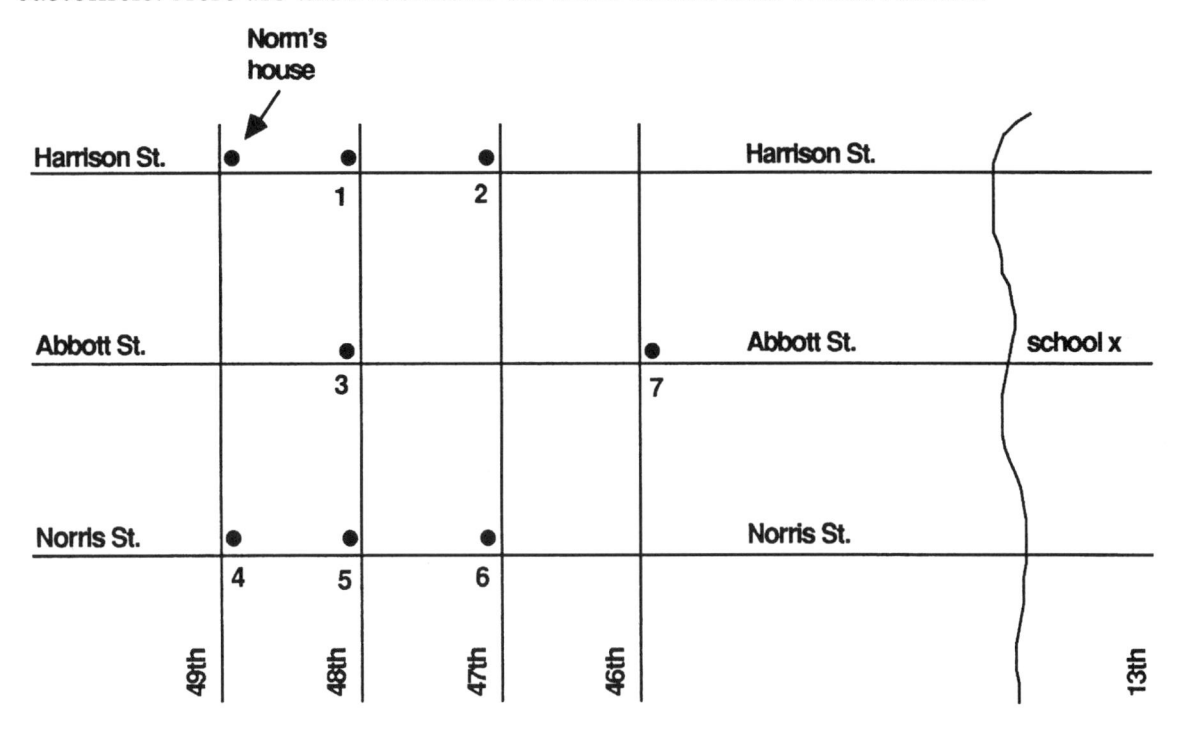

```
                Norm's
                house
                  ↓
Harrison St.      •     •         •          |  Harrison St.        |
                        1         2                                 |
                                                                    |
                                                                    |
Abbott St.              •                •   |  Abbott St.          |  school x
                        3                7                          |
                                                                    |
                                                                    |
Norris St.        •     •         •          |  Norris St.          |
                  4     5         6                                 |
                 49th  48th      47th       46th                   13th
```

The numbers mark the houses Norm serves and the order in which he delivers his eggs.

For each customer Norm has built a little box, much like the kind people used to have when milkmen delivered their milk. He carefully stacks the seven dozen eggs in a cart that he pulls with his bicycle and then puts a carton with a dozen eggs in each box on the way to his school on Abbott Street.

Everything works out very well for Norm for several months. He is never late to school, even though he has a mile to go after he has delivered eggs to his last customer. After things have gone so well, however, a snag develops. Two families complain about Norm's taking a shortcut through their properties, and he has to figure out how he can deliver his eggs in the same amount of time without taking the shortcuts.

What should his new route be? You can find his original route simply by connecting the dots in order on the map above. Draw in the best alternative route for Norm to take so that he can still get to school on time.

Cognitive Connections © 1996 Zephyr Press, Tucson, Arizona

45 A Gem of an Idea

Let's suppose that a violent volcanic eruption occurred in the south Pacific Ocean, producing not only lava and ash but some surprising debris. Because of the location of this volcano in the ocean—where there were no islands before this eruption created one—some of the minerals in this area are unknown. When scientists are finally able to land on the island and explore it, they find huge rocks whose surfaces are dotted with color. The colors are remarkable, so the scientists begin carefully cutting up the rocks.

The rocks yield gems extraordinary in their brilliant colors; they are in unusual hues almost never seen in gems before. The gems are generally in two forms: hexagonal crystals (four axes with three of them at right angles) and tetragonal crystals (three axes at right angles).

Draw one hexagonal gem and one tetragonal gem that the scientists might have discovered, giving each an unusual and beautiful color. You may want to review the shapes of crystals in a reference book before you begin. A protractor will also be useful.

46 Mowing 'Em Down

Harry's power lawn mower breaks down, and he doesn't want to spend the money to have it repaired again. The last time he took it to the shop he paid $80, and it was useless in little more than a month. The only genuine alternative is to use the old, rusty hand mower that Harry bought at a thrift store for a few dollars. It isn't working very well either, but the recent spell of good weather has made the lawn shaggy. Harry knows if he waits any longer, his wife will become more unhappy with him and the grass will be even more difficult to cut.

So Harry drags the hand mower out of the shed and tries to cut the front lawn. The steep slope almost defeats him. With a power mower, he can go in parallel lines. But with the hand mower, Harry can't really manage going back and forth when he reaches the slope. Then he tries going up and down, and that is worse.

How can Harry solve his problem without resorting to buying another mower? List all of the solutions you can think of, and give illustrations in the space below.

47 Kitchen Design

This illustration is of a typical kitchen clock. Its face is round, but some kitchen clocks have faces that are square or even hexagonal. What is the shape of the clock in your kitchen? Draw a picture of it.

IT'S COOKIE-BAKING TIME!

In your kitchen, what shape is the work-area countertop? Draw a picture or diagram of it.

Could the shape of the countertop be changed? If so, would the new shape be more efficient? Show how you would design it, and tell what advantages there would be to the shape.

(Continued)

Name _____

What is the shape of your sink? Draw a picture or a diagram of it. Could its shape be changed? How could it be changed? Draw a diagram of it. With its new shape, would your kitchen sink be more efficient? If so, how would it be more efficient?

What shape is the overhead light fixture in the kitchen? Draw a picture or a diagram of it. Would it be more efficient or attractive if it had another shape? What shape would that be, and why would it be more efficient or attractive?

What is the shape of the top of the range? Draw a picture or a diagram of it. Could the shape of the top of the range be changed so that it would be more convenient or efficient? If so, draw a diagram of how it could look. Explain how it could be more convenient or efficient.

Are there some items in the kitchen whose shapes can't be changed? If so, which ones are they and why can't they be changed? Draw them and explain.

Cognitive Connections © 1996 Zephyr Press, Tucson, Arizona

Name _____

48 Going Around

A. If you have something—let's say a quarter-inch thick piece of plywood—that has the shape of a circle, and you rotate it on end on the ground (or floor), what happens? Make it any convenient diameter.

_____
_____
_____

What happens if you rotate it in water?

_____
_____
_____

What happens if you push it forward or backward in the water without rotating it?

_____
_____
_____

What can be done with that plywood circle? Name as many uses as you can for just the plywood circle itself.

_____
_____
_____
_____

(Continued)

B. What if the shape is not a circle but an equilateral triangle about the same size as the circle? What happens if you rotate it on the ground?

_____
_____
_____
_____
_____

What happens if you rotate it in water?

_____
_____
_____
_____

What happens if you push it forward or backward in the water without rotating it?

_____
_____
_____
_____

What can be done with that plywood triangle? Name as many uses as you can for just the plywood triangle.

_____
_____
_____
_____
_____

(Continued)

Name _____

C. What if the shape is a hexagon the same size as the circle? What happens if you rotate it on the ground?

_____
_____
_____
_____

What happens if you rotate it in water?

_____
_____
_____
_____

What happens if you push it forward or backward in the water without rotating it?

_____
_____
_____
_____

In all of these movements, does the hexagon differ from the circle and the triangle? How does it differ from each?

_____
_____
_____
_____
_____
_____

(Continued)

Name _____

D. If you have a chance, try fastening two of the shapes together. Then rotate them in air and water. Push them forward and backward in water. Report what happens in the following space.

49 Count the Ways

A. Four high school students, who don't know each other too well because they are in different grades, live near one another in an apartment complex. They live about a mile from their high school.

Sarah, who is in the tenth grade, leaves for school a little before the others. The route she takes gets her to the front door of the high school in seventeen minutes. The other three take different routes. Harry, a junior, takes nineteen minutes to reach the school; Nancy, a senior, takes sixteen minutes; and Marvin, a freshman, doesn't reach school for twenty minutes. Why the differences in the time it takes them to get to school?

Here is a map of the high school and surrounding neighborhood. Actually, it is a segment of the standard city map. After thinking about the four students and how long it takes them to reach the school, examine the map and then come up with at least four hypotheses to account for the differences in time the four students take to get to school.

(Continued)

Name _____

Hypothesis 1: _____
_____
_____

Hypothesis 2: _____
_____
_____

Hypothesis 3: _____
_____
_____

Hypothesis 4: _____
_____
_____

Other hypotheses: _____
_____
_____

B. How long will it be before the time it takes for each student to reach school changes?
_____
_____

Why do you think so?
_____
_____
_____
_____
_____
_____

Name _____

50 What's the Angle?

Mr. Jasper is in a bind. He has to remove that old elm tree by five o'clock or the city will do it for him and give him a big bill. There have been a number of complaints that the diseased elm might soon fall, thus creating a hazard to passers-by and motorists. Mr. Jasper was called out of town on urgent business the day before, but the fact is he's procrastinated about cutting down the tree. He has a chain saw, and he knows how to fell a tree, but he doesn't know how high the tree is so he can't determine how far it will fall in the desired direction.

Mr. Jasper knows a little about finding the height of something by determining the angle of the top from a point so many feet from the base. But all he has is his son's protractor for measuring the angle, and it is now four-thirty. He lives on the edge of town, and it's a fifteen-minute drive to a store where he could get the proper instrument for measuring the angle. What should he do?

_____
_____
_____
_____
_____
_____
_____
_____

Is there something else he might do?
_____
_____

What is the formula for determining the height of the tree Mr. Jasper wants to cut down?
_____
_____

Name _____

51 Configurations

Abstract painters, graphics artists, architects, and home decorators are fond of combining geometrical shapes. Here is a familiar one.

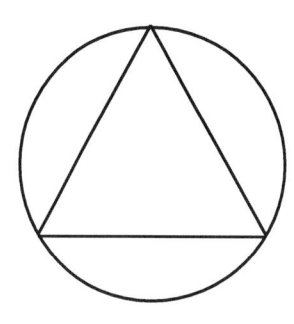

Have you seen it anywhere? _____ If so, where? _____
_____

Does it have a name? _____ If so, what is it called? _____
_____

Here is a hexagon.

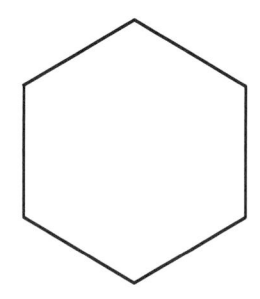

Try combining it with other geometric shapes. After you have come up with one you like, draw it and name it.

(Continued)

Cognitive Connections © 1996 Zephyr Press, Tucson, Arizona

Name _____

This is a pentagon.

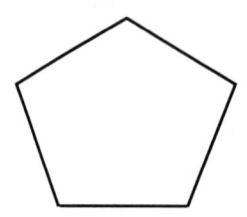

With what geometric shapes could it be combined? Try several and then draw the one you like best and name it.

This is an octagon.

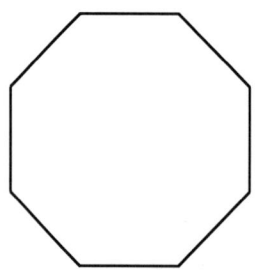

What geometric shapes can be combined with it? Try several and then draw the one you like best. Name it.

52 Parts

A. Here are some common questions math teachers ask:

 1. How many quarters does it take to make a half?

 2. Which is greater, three-fifths or two-thirds?

 3. How many sixths are there in a whole, or 1?

 4. How much greater is 1 than 7/8?

 5. If Bill and Fritz together have twelve baseball cards and Fritz has two-thirds of them, how many baseball cards does Fritz have?

 What do all of these questions have in common?

 _____
 _____
 _____
 _____

B. Develop three other questions that are concerned with the same mathematical topic.

 _____
 _____
 _____
 _____
 _____
 _____
 _____
 _____
 _____
 _____

53 Equal Parts

A. James, a fifth-grader, is asked to organize the school play in the spring. His job is to get volunteers from the third, fourth, and fifth grades to participate in the play. Some of the students will be acting, others will handle the props and scenery, and one or two will be responsible for the actors' makeup. James thinks he'll have quite a few volunteers, but after going to all of the classes twice and pleading for participants, he is only able to get four third-graders, four fourth-graders, and three fifth-graders to volunteer.

By tradition, each of the three classes has an equal number of participants in the school play; that is, one-third of the participants come from each of the classes. It seems to James that he doesn't have enough volunteers to uphold the tradition. When James talks to Mrs. Norris about the situation, she tells him that he will be able to figure out a way to maintain the tradition. James protests, but Mrs. Norris says, "There are at least two ways—maybe more—to make it work."

B. If Mrs. Norris is correct, show how James can get equal numbers from each class to participate in the school play. There is an obvious solution, but also try to come up with others that will satisfy the requirement of equal numbers of participants from the three classes. Explain your solution.

_____
_____
_____
_____

Name _____

54 Percentage Baseball

Your favorite baseball team has won ten games and lost six, but it is eager to raise its record to .750 (75 percent). How many games will it have to win in a row to have a .750 record of wins and losses?

How could this information help your team?

_____
_____
_____
_____
_____
_____
_____
_____
_____
_____

55 Tracy Figures

These figures are a record of Tracy's income and outgo for two weeks last summer. Tracy lives in a state that doesn't have a sales tax.

```
     10                        10
      4.95                      1.05
      1.25                      4.99
      3.80                      5.00
             -.50
```

Give a plausible description for each item in the two columns. In particular, tell what the last figure indicates.

10 _____   10 _____

    4.95 _____   1.05 _____

    1.25 _____   4.99 _____

    3.80 _____   5.00 _____

          -.50 _____

Do you have any advice for Tracy? Write it in the space below.

_____
_____
_____
_____
_____
_____
_____
_____
_____
_____

56 Sprouts

A. Robert likes to garden, but he isn't very good at it. Usually he has problems with insects attacking his vegetables, and a good proportion of his seeds don't germinate. This year he plants twenty-six beet seeds, and fifteen sprout. He plants thirty carrot seeds, and twenty-five sprout. Something goes wrong with the onions; only eight of twenty-four sprout. Robert is luckier with cucumbers—of the 22 seeds he plants, 20 sprout.

What percentage of his beets germinate? (Round off to 2 places.) _____

What percentage of his carrots germinate? _____

What percentage of his onions sprout? _____

What percentage of his cucumbers germinate? _____

(Continued)

Name _____

Overall, what percentage of Robert's seeds germinate? _____

Should you calculate a percentage of the four percentages to get the answer? _____ Why or why not?
_____
_____
_____

B. Mathematically, is there another way to look at Robert's success in getting his seeds to sprout? _____ What is it?
_____
_____
_____

88 Cognitive Connections © 1996 Zephyr Press, Tucson, Arizona

Name _____

57 Twice as Much

A. Ratios are relationships. One dictionary says a ratio is "a fixed relation in degree, number, etc., between two similar things." For example, if you were so disposed, you could compare the red checks to the white checks on a checkered tablecloth and come up with a ratio. Do you suppose that it would be 1:1?

Find the ratios for these everyday situations:

1. The number of boys versus that of girls participating in after-school sports. _____

2. The number of students in a class whose hair styles cover their ears as opposed to those with uncovered ears. _____

3. Two brands of computers in school (or two models if there is only one brand). _____

4. Your weekly average hours asleep and awake for a day. _____

5. The number of carpeted rooms as opposed to rooms without carpets in your home. _____

6. The number of students in your class who eat one thing at a time for lunch and the number who go from portion to portion of various dishes. _____

7. The number of your teeth without fillings compared to those with fillings. Does this ratio tell you what percentage of teeth has fillings? _____ Why or why not?

_____

_____

_____

_____

(Continued)

Cognitive Connections © 1996 Zephyr Press, Tucson, Arizona

B. We can usually see relationships between pairs of things that can be put in the same classifications, and these relationships can often be expressed as ratios. See how many ratios you can find in these two paragraphs.

The bicycle is the favorite mode of transportation in many urban areas of Europe. In one city there are four times as many people riding bicycles to work as there are driving cars and twice as many as are on foot. It is unclear if the health benefits of bike riding outweigh those of walking, but in that city incidents of heart problems among the bike riders are half those of the car drivers and riders.

Of course one of the greatest benefits from riding bicycles and walking is the fact that those activities don't pollute the air. Estimates of the causes of air pollution in the same city indicate that 240 times as much nitrogen dioxide is caused by factory emissions as is caused by internal combustion engines. About 595 times as much carbon dioxide is sent into the air as a result of factory emissions as is released by internal combustion engines (principally cars) in the same city.

Ratios you found in the two paragraphs:

_____

_____

If there are approximately 70,000 workers in that city, about how many go to work in cars?

_____

(Continued)

C. What ratios could you find that would give us important information in these areas of concern?

- The depletion of the ozone layer in the stratosphere

- Increasing overpopulation in third world countries

- The U.S. trade deficit

- The decreasing number of doctors practicing in rural areas

Name _____

58 Getting Smaller

A. During the past two or three decades one trend in the marketing of consumer goods has become apparent to all of us—the packages (or their contents) are getting smaller and the prices are getting bigger. When manufacturers want to increase their profit, they often will reduce the size of a commodity (such as a candy bar) but not raise the price. We simply get less for our money. Manufacturers maintain that their costs of doing business have increased more and more, so they have no choice other than to reduce the size of the product or raise its price.

WOULD YOU BELIEVE MY ANCESTORS WERE FOUR-POUNDERS AND COST LESS, TOO?

What items during your life have become smaller while the price remained the same? Name at least five.

1. _____
2. _____
3. _____
4. _____
5. _____

Determine the percentage of shrinkage with the last change for each item, and put that percentage next to the item.

What items during your lifetime have stayed the same size but have become more expensive? Name at least five.

1. _____
2. _____
3. _____
4. _____
5. _____

Determine the percentage of increase in their most recent price changes. Put that percentage next to the item.

(Continued)

B. Since you can't do very much about inflation, you don't have many options when it comes to purchasing the items you've listed. There are ways of coping with smaller commodities and higher prices, however. Select one of the items in your first list of shrinking sizes and work out a strategy for dealing with the smaller size. Do the same for dealing with one item that now costs more.

Smaller Size Strategy: _____

_____

_____

_____

_____

_____

_____

_____

Higher Price Strategy: _____

_____

_____

_____

_____

_____

_____

_____

59 More Stop than Go

A. Doug's father is an impatient man. He drives to work the same way every morning, Monday through Friday, and is often annoyed that he has to stop his car at the traffic light three blocks from his home. The light is at an intersection of the main street going through town and a residential street close to where Doug's family lives. After having to stop at the intersection two consecutive mornings, Doug's father decides to record how many times he can cross without stopping and how many times he has to stop at the signal. He guesses that he has to stop four times more often than he is able to drive through.

Here is the record of what happens for two weeks:

Monday—stops	Monday—goes through
Tuesday—stops	Tuesday—stops
Wednesday—goes through	Wednesday—goes through
Thursday—stops	Thursday—stops
Friday—stops	Friday—stops

Is Doug's father correct about the ratio of times he stops to the times he doesn't? _____

What is the percentage? _____

(Continued)

Name _____

B. Does the data Doug's father acquire prove anything? Explain.

_____
_____
_____
_____
_____
_____

C. Does Doug's father have enough information to come to a valid conclusion? _____

What can he do with the information he has now?

_____
_____
_____
_____
_____
_____
_____
_____
_____
_____
_____
_____

Cognitive Connections © 1996 Zephyr Press, Tucson, Arizona

Name _____

"How's the Weather Up There?"

A. Basketball players are getting taller and taller. A few decades ago there was only one seven-foot-tall player playing organized basketball in North America. Now it seems there are seven-footers playing for every professional and college team. A player who stood 6'3" was one of the tallest, if not the tallest, player on a high school team in 1940. Now he would be one of the shortest.

    A college team whose players are average in height might have a center at 6'11", forwards at 6'9" and 6'7", and guards at 6'5" and 6'3". What is their average height? _____ What is the average height of the starting five of the college or university nearest you? _____

    What is the reason for this tremendous increase in the height of basketball players?

    _____
    _____
    _____

B. Will basketball players keep getting taller? Calculate the rate at which basketball teams have increased in height over the past fifty years. (A high school or college yearbook may give you the information.) Then project how tall the average player will be fifty years from now if that rate continues constant.

Cognitive Connections © 1996 Zephyr Press, Tucson, Arizona

Name _____

61 The Puddlejumpers and Puffers Parade

A. A big event in Hending each year is the 10,000-meter road race that has been nicknamed "The Puddlejumpers and Puffers Parade." The original—and official—name is the Annual Hending-Barlow County 10,000-Meter Road Race. Runners of all ages are welcome to compete, and prizes are given in three age groups:

> Group A: up through 31 years of age
>
> Group B: 32 through 40 years
>
> Group C: 41 years and older

No distinctions are made between male and female runners.

Not everyone finishes the race, however. Some of the contestants each year overestimate the shape their bodies are in. Last year four times as many runners in Group A than those in Group C finished. One-third as many runners in Group C than those in Group B finished.

If 152 runners finished the race, how many of Group B were able to complete the race? _____

(Continued)

Cognitive Connections © 1996 Zephyr Press, Tucson, Arizona

Name _____

B. Tom Rezik, one of the organizers of the meet, doesn't like handing out duplicate sets of prizes to the first three finishers of each group. Every year he fusses about the winner of Group C getting as nice a prize as the winner of Group A, even if the Group A winner finishes twenty minutes ahead of his or her older rival. He thinks the prize-giving and the race should be conducted differently. His suggestions, so far, have fallen on the deaf ears of his fellow committee members.

On the other hand, maybe Tom just hasn't come up with a fair way to adjust for the wide range of abilities of the runners. He says he can think of other sports that "even out the competition and make the prizes really mean something." What sports does he have in mind? Sports with handicaps? How would you change the race to accommodate Tom but still make the prizes satisfy everyone?

_____
_____
_____
_____
_____
_____
_____
_____
_____
_____
_____
_____
_____
_____
_____
_____
_____

62 Less than $10.00

Although it may be hard for you to believe, there are times in one's life when a knowledge of algebra comes in handy. For simple, everyday problems, algebra helps you get answers quickly. For instance, if a store advertises that a $216 bicycle can be purchased for half down and the balance in 12 monthly payments, with $6.00 interest charges, you can find out how much the monthly payments will be by using algebra.

$$\frac{\$216}{2} = \$108 \qquad \frac{\$108 + \$6}{12} = x$$

$$\frac{114}{12} = x$$

$$\$9.50 = x$$

The monthly payments will be $9.50. (For this example, we'll imagine that the purchase is being made in a state where people pay no sales tax.)

Let's say that you have watched a friend doing some figuring on a scrap of paper for about five minutes. She then walks away, leaving the paper behind. Here is what you find on the scrap of paper.

$$\$20 \times n = \$195 \times .9$$

$$\$20 \times n = \$195$$
$$\times .9$$
$$\$175.50$$

$$\frac{20 \times n}{20} = \frac{\$175.50}{\$20}$$

$$n = 8.7 \quad \text{about 9 with tax}$$

What do you think the calculations were all about? What does the "n" represent?

_____
_____
_____
_____
_____

63 Multiple Distributions

Let's suppose that you are a teacher of beginning algebra. You would like to introduce the distributive law to your students. It can be represented in this way:

$$a(b + c) = ab + ac$$

You have a class of diverse students, so you decide you had better come up with a number of ways to present the distributive law, including approaches that use manipulatives as well as the chalkboard. Describe as many ways as you can think of for presenting the distributive law to your students.

64 Nine Left

Vincent goes to the stockyards in his pickup truck on Thursday. He finds that the pens are nearly empty; only nine steers are there.

Vincent wants to have his steers added to the group that is being fattened up, but he doesn't see the man with whom he usually deals anywhere. So he goes into the room that serves as an office adjacent to the pens. When he enters, he sees a piece of paper pinned to the wall. Following is what Vincent reads on the paper:

$$\frac{1}{12} = \frac{75}{x}$$

$$x = 900$$

Apr.

$$\begin{array}{r} 75 \\ \times 12 \\ \hline 150 \\ 750 \\ \hline 900 \end{array}$$

$$75 - 9 = 66$$

$$\begin{array}{r} 900 \\ -66 \\ \hline 834 \end{array}$$

What do you think the figures represent? _____

_____

_____

What is the problem that someone—probably the man Vincent has been dealing with—was figuring out? _____

_____

_____

Explain what each of the figures and "Apr." represent. _____

_____

_____

_____

_____

_____

Cognitive Connections © 1996 Zephyr Press, Tucson, Arizona

65 Story Problems

A. Do you prefer to do a full page of multiplication algorisms over a couple of "word problems"? If so, why do you prefer the repetition and relative monotony of doing the algorisms?

_____

_____

The process of solving a word, or story, problem, is generally to find the basic elements and represent them in an algorism. For example, let's say the problem is about a farmer wondering how he can increase his hens' production of eggs to seventy dozen a week if he adds to his flock of 96 hens, and each hen now averages one egg per day. If the student is successful, he or she sees that the operations involved in solving the problem are finding out how many eggs are now being produced by the hens, that is, multiplication; how many more are needed, that is, subtraction; and how many more hens are needed, that is, division. There are three algorisms for the student to do in order to solve the problem. (How many more hens does the farmer have to acquire, assuming that the new hens also produce one egg per day?)

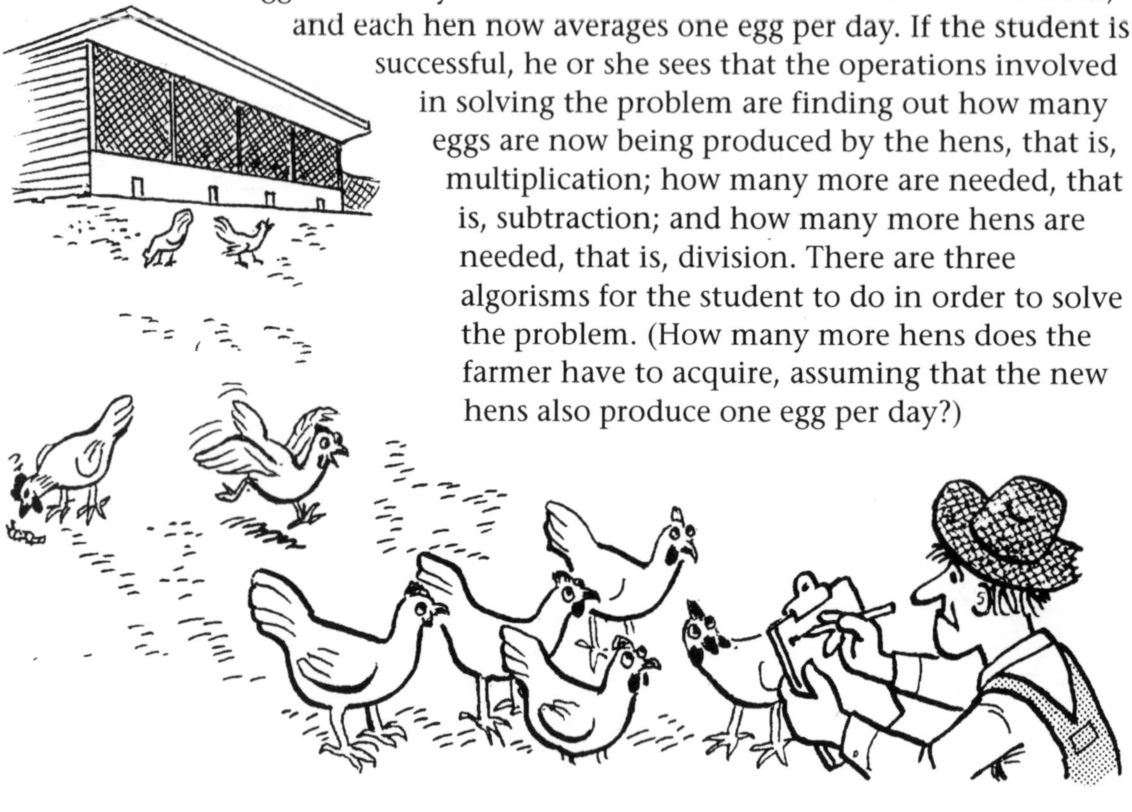

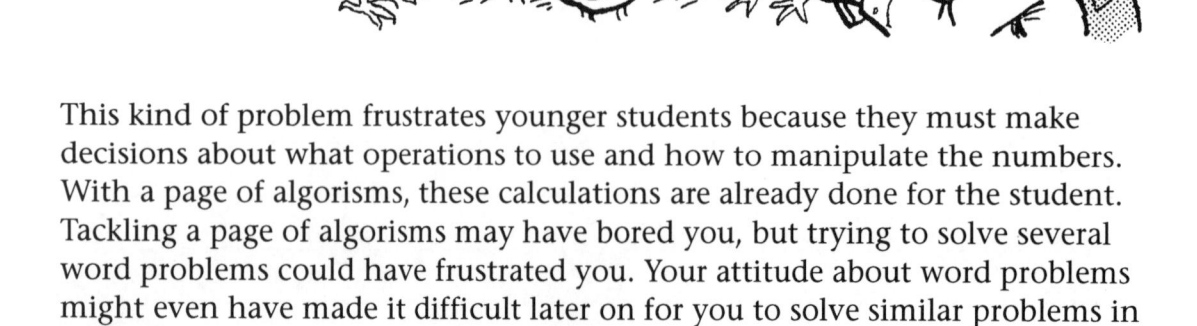

This kind of problem frustrates younger students because they must make decisions about what operations to use and how to manipulate the numbers. With a page of algorisms, these calculations are already done for the student. Tackling a page of algorisms may have bored you, but trying to solve several word problems could have frustrated you. Your attitude about word problems might even have made it difficult later on for you to solve similar problems in other disciplines or in real-life situations.

(Continued)

102 Cognitive Connections © 1996 Zephyr Press, Tucson, Arizona

B. Why don't we reverse the process? Take the algorism below and create a word problem that fits it. This exercise may make word problems seem slightly less distasteful to you.

$$x - \frac{1}{3}x = 64 + 12$$

The Sketch

Here is a sketch. It was found on the desk of a ten-year-old boy.

```
        5
    ┌───────┬───────┐
    │       │       │
    │   C   │   D   │ 5
    │       │       │
    ├───────┼───────┤
    │       │       │
    │   B   │   A  ╱│
    │       │  ╱   │
    └───────┴───────┘
```

What do the numbers mean? _____

_____

What does the "A" mean? _____

_____

What do the other letters mean? _____

_____

_____

What is the sketch all about? _____

_____

Would you add anything to it? _____ If not, why not? _____

_____

_____

(Continued)

104 Cognitive Connections © 1996 Zephyr Press, Tucson, Arizona

Name _____

What other use could be made of this sketch? _____
_____
_____

If you would like, add some numbers and lines to the sketch. Then describe what the sketch you have drawn shows. Tell about it in the space below.

67 It Figures

A. Although it may not be apparent to you now, mathematics has become the second most important tool to anyone entering the job market. What is the most important tool for someone seeking a job?

___

Obviously, some jobs require more mathematical skills than others. Select one from each of these pairs of jobs as the one requiring more mathematical knowledge and skills, and explain why it requires them. Be specific about the knowledge and skills needed. If you need more information, look into reference books and talk to occupational counselors.

1. on-flight airline attendant or librarian ___

2. high school track coach or janitor ___

3. retail sales clerk or bank teller ___

4. casino blackjack dealer or garage mechanic ___

(Continued)

Name _____

5. surveyor or carpenter _____
   _____
   _____
   _____

6. executive secretary or farmer _____
   _____
   _____
   _____

7. electrical engineer or computer programmer _____
   _____
   _____
   _____

B. What is your ultimate occupational goal? _____

Will it require any mathematical skills? _____ Will it require any math skills you don't have now? _____ If so, how will you acquire these skills?

_____
_____
_____
_____
_____
_____
_____
_____
_____

68 Four Plus Seven Make Nine

Christine needs to bake some cookies in exactly nine continuous minutes, but none of her clocks work because they are electronic and there has just been a power outage. The clocks just blink at her, and she doesn't know how to restart them. She has two egg timers, though. One measures four minutes, and the second measures seven minutes. There are no graduations on the egg timers, so she can't guess when an egg timer is half finished. What is the quickest way Christine can measure nine minutes with the two timers?

You can do your figuring and drawing in the space below.

69 Mel Comes Through

Mel had a bad day at school, and he isn't talking to anyone. His dad can't get him to talk about sports. His older brother, T. J., can't get him to talk about cars. Even his mother can't get Mel to say anything when she tells him about dinner. And pizza is Mel's favorite dinner.

It is mostly his arithmetic that is bothering Mel. He doesn't remember the combinations very well. Not very well at all. Flash cards haven't helped. Nothing helps. Mel doesn't want to go to school tomorrow and not know the answers again. He even considers pretending to be sick so he can stay home.

Mel does go to school the next day. And it is a very good day. What's more, Mel does it all himself. He likes his teacher, but he thinks she is tired of helping him. Mel doesn't want to admit to any of his classmates that he wants help from them.

He says to himself, "I can go somewhere else in school to get better in my arithmetic. There is something else I can do. I'm just not looking around enough. I'm not using my head."

Where does Mel go, and what does he do? He finds his help right in school when he thinks of all the resources, physical and human, that a school has. What do you think Mel does?

70 How Do You Poach a Roach?

A. People like rhymes, and rhymes often pop up in our conversations. Some, such as the familiar, "See you later, alligator," are overused. It's unlikely, however, that you hear a lot of rhyming in your math class. It might happen occasionally, as when a teacher asks, "How would you divide the side?" But it wouldn't happen very often.

Following are some rhymes that you probably won't hear in class. Would it be possible to

1. add a pad? How would you do it?

2. number some lumber? How would you do that?

3. calculate a skate? How would you do that?

4. divide a ride? How could that be done?

5. meter a bleater? How would you do that?

6. square a pear? How could that be done?

7. curve a nerve? How could that be done?

8. quarter a mortar? How would you do that?

9. compound a mound? How would you do that?

(Continued)

Name _____

10. arc a lark? How could that be accomplished?

B. How can you half a calf without harming it?

C. See if you can come up with other rhymes that show how people might possibly interact with animals. For example, how do you poach a roach or deter a cur? Answer your own questions.

71 A Square Inch

A. Louis and Douglas have an argument. Louis claims that he has more freckles than Douglas has. A redhead, Douglas has always been proud of his freckles. When he was very little, Douglas's mother told him that the extra pigmentation in his skin is a sign that some of his goodness has leaked and is showing on his skin. Douglas has unshakable faith in his mother's pronouncements.

Louis, on the other hand, has never felt very good about the specks of reddish-brown on his body. He doesn't like being one of the few kids in school who are covered with freckles. He had measles in elementary school, and the teacher sent him home when she noticed his droopiness. She said, "Goodness! I didn't notice those splotches. They got lost among all those freckles." That embarrassed Louis, who was sometimes called "Speckles."

Louis got into the argument about who has the most freckles because he thinks he sees an opportunity to win some money in a bet. Since Douglas is so proud of his freckles, it isn't hard to entice him into a bet.

They decide that, since it is nearly impossible to count all the freckles on their faces, a sample will be taken from each face. They will measure one square inch and photograph the inch with Leonard's father's camera, which has a lens capable of focusing on very small subjects. Three people will count the freckles in each square inch. To make it fair, each boy is heavily blindfolded (to protect his eyes), and his chosen "second" is also blindfolded. The second then lightly touches the face of his friend, as in "Blind Man's Bluff," with the eraser of a pencil in order to designate the area to be measured. The second for Douglas hits his cheek. The second for Louis touches his nose.

Following are the results of their findings:

Judge	A Square Inch of Louis's Face	A Square Inch of Douglas's Face
Monica	17	25
Theresa	21	29
Izzy	15	30

(Continued)

Name _____

B. What are the average counts for each? Why do the counts differ? Do you see any tendencies among the judges? _____ If so, what are they?

_____
_____
_____
_____
_____

C. As a sampling technique, did this plan have any problems?

_____
_____
_____

In the field of statistics, is this procedure a legitimate one? _____ What is the margin of error in such a sampling?

_____
_____
_____

Would the square inch chosen really be representative of the total number of freckles on each boy's face? _____ If yes, why do you think so?

_____
_____
_____

Would you change the procedure in any way? _____ If so, what would you do differently?

_____
_____
_____
_____

72 Calculating by Hand

A. You probably use the arithmetic operation, division, more often than you realize. Whenever you separate something in halves, you are dividing; whenever you average two or more figures you are also dividing.

Give two examples of the use of division on the playground.

_____
_____
_____
_____
_____
_____
_____

Give two other instances when you use division during a normal day.

_____
_____
_____
_____
_____
_____
_____

(Continued)

Name _____

B. Many careful shoppers carry a calculator with them when they go shopping. They can determine whether the larger of two sizes is a genuine bargain by dividing the prices of the items by their quantities. For many years now purses have been fitted with calculators so that people can make comparisons when they shop (and also find out if they are overdrawn on their checking accounts).

What other uses are there for carrying a calculator? Name as many as you can think of.

73 Yebas for Dollars

A. Let's suppose you are an explorer and you somehow discover an ancient city in a very remote mountainous area. To your astonishment, when you enter the large city, the people, although dressed differently than any you have ever seen, seem to be products of a civilization equal or superior to yours. They receive you and your party courteously. Because of the altitude, the climate is mild. Agricultural products are varied, but there are no tropical fruits. The people have domesticated animals similar to yours. Because of their advanced technology, the people seem to be able to produce more than enough food by means of hydroponics and other methods. Moreover, they can manufacture everything they need for housing, transportation, and industry.

In spite of language differences you learn that the people of the city have a monetary system that is simple but highly efficient. As is the case in Japan, there is only one unit of exchange. The *yeba* is the basic unit. After becoming friendly with the inhabitants of the city and gaining their trust, you determine the prices of some basic commodities and services. A container of milk (which doesn't come from a cow) is priced at 105 yebas; the container looks to be about the size and capacity of a quart. A boy's shirt costs 500 yebas; it is beautifully made and has a colorful design. What looks to be a kitchen knife is offered for sale at 450 yebas. A street cleaner earns 725 yebas an hour, and the streets are very clean. A banker earns 32,000 yebas a week.

(Continued)

Name _____

From the information you have acquired about the prices of commodities and services, you believe you can make up a conversion table of yebas and dollars that will give you an idea of the relative costs of goods and services in comparison with those back home. Fortunately for you, the people have the same decimal system of enumeration that we have.

Decide what denominations these people are using for their money and of what metals their coins are comprised. Then make up a table showing equivalent values for their money and ours. (For example, a dime is equal to ? yebas.)

B. What would you suppose the going price in yebas is for the following items and services:

	yebas		yebas
1. small bar of soap	_____	8. rent for one-family dwelling	_____
2. medium-size sack of flour	_____	9. flutelike musical instrument	_____
3. hourly wage of farm laborer	_____	10. straw broom	_____
4. pair of heavy stockings	_____	11. hourly wage of plumber	_____
5. bundle of firewood	_____	12. ceramic mixing bowl	_____
6. small sack of salt	_____	13. bag of candy	_____
7. girl's skirt	_____	14. man's pants	_____

Cognitive Connections © 1996 Zephyr Press, Tucson, Arizona

Name _____

74 Back to the Basics

Following is a possible headline in the *Chicago Tribune*:

Worldwide Conspiracy Shuts Down All Computers

It finally happens. After years of worrying about computer viruses that could cause unimagined harm to computer networks all over the world, a worldwide conspiracy succeeds in damaging every memory bank and program on the planet! Restoring service will take months.

What will the computer technicians and programmers do now?

_____
_____
_____
_____
_____

What will mathematicians in the following places do?

1. In government offices?

   _____
   _____
   _____
   _____
   _____

(Continued)

Name _____

2. In industries such as banking and insurance?

_____
_____
_____
_____
_____
_____

3. In universities carrying on applied and pure research?

_____
_____
_____
_____
_____
_____

List at least three benefits of this catastrophe.

_____
_____
_____
_____
_____
_____
_____
_____

Name _____

75 Experimenting with Humor

You have probably done some experiments in school. You may have done experiments with fertilized eggs or sprouting beans. You may have even performed experiments in a social studies class. Here is a chance, however, to do an experiment that promises a little entertainment. Like any good experiment, you won't know how it will come out until you do it.

Two jokes are listed below. Tell them to your friends in approximately the same words as they are written. Predict on a four-point scale how your friends will react to the jokes. Don't tell your friends that they are part of an experiment, and don't let them see you writing anything after you tell the jokes.

Make a decision as to how close you should be in your predictions if you know your friends pretty well. An average difference of ±1 for the ten subjects might be outstanding. Then determine the average difference between your predictions and the actual reactions of your friends for each joke. Compare those differences with your criterion. For example, your predictions average 3.2 for the first joke and the average scores are 1.5. Your criterion for coming close to guessing the reactions is a difference of ±1. The actual difference was −1.7, so you didn't meet the criterion.

SCHEME FOR SCORING

Negative Reaction	—	0
No Reaction at All	—	1
Mild Laughter	—	2
Spontaneous Laughter	—	3

JOKE 1

In Bratislava, Czechoslovakia, the favorite butt of jokes is the Skoda, a tinny car manufactured right outside of town. A fellow goes into a parts stores and asks, "Can I get a gas cap for a Skoda?" and the guy behind the counter says, "Seems like a fair trade to me."

JOKE 2

The bank of a little village in Nebraska failed, and there was a chance that the community would not survive. One man, who had been out of town when the bank failed, called a friend and said: "How is everyone in town taking it, Eric?" "Well," Eric replied, "the biggest problem is that since there are no two-story buildings in town, everyone's trying to kill themselves by jumping off the curb!"

(These two jokes came from an article by Roger L. Welsch, who writes for *Natural History*.)

(Continued)

Name _____

RESULTS OF EXPERIMENT

	Name	JOKE 1 Score	Prediction	JOKE 2 Score	Prediction
Subject 1	_____	____	____	____	____
Subject 2	_____	____	____	____	____
Subject 3	_____	____	____	____	____
Subject 4	_____	____	____	____	____
Subject 5	_____	____	____	____	____
Subject 6	_____	____	____	____	____
Subject 7	_____	____	____	____	____
Subject 8	_____	____	____	____	____
Subject 9	_____	____	____	____	____
Subject 10	_____	____	____	____	____

Cognitive Connections © 1996 Zephyr Press, Tucson, Arizona

76 Profits

Using any appropriate mathematical tools, predict the profits of a small women's clothing store during the three fall months of September, October, and November in these categories: sports apparel, winter coats and jackets, bridal gowns, ready-to-wear, and accessories.

Following are the figures for sales and profits in the previous year:

	Previous Year's Sales for Sept., Oct., and Nov.	Previous Year's Profits for Sept., Oct., and Nov.
sports apparel	$ 2504.80	$ 175.34
winter coats and jackets	3792.50	303.40
bridal gowns	2150.00	193.50
ready-to-wear	8533.90	597.37
accessories	1896.75	151.74

(A number of other categories are not included in this list of the store's sales.)

Take into consideration as many factors as you can in making your predictions, for example, current and projected state of the national economy, current and projected state of the local economy (make it your own area's economy), current and projected employment figures for the area, projected costs of garments (whether the price of goods is rising or falling according to demand for certain fashions), and the like.

You'll have to do a little research in order to make your predictions, and you might interview a shop owner, who also must do some research in estimating purchases and sales in doing business.

(Continued)

Name _____

Use the listing below to make your predictions.

Your Predictions

	Sales for Sept., Oct., and Nov.	Profits for Sept., Oct., and Nov.
sports apparel	_____	_____
winter coats and jackets	_____	_____
bridal gowns	_____	_____
ready-to-wear	_____	_____
accessories	_____	_____

77 It's Easy Venn You Know How

A. Venn diagrams are probably the most useful tools in set theory. An English scholar, John Venn, began using rectangles as well as circles to represent sets in 1894. Since then the diagrams that bear his name have served mathematicians quite well. Below is an example of a Venn diagram.

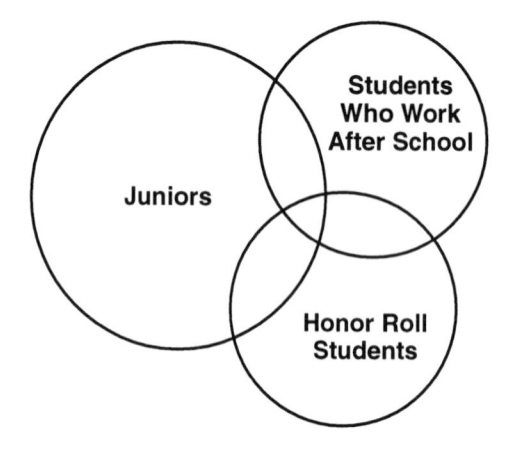

(Venn diagram with three overlapping circles labeled "Juniors," "Students Who Work After School," and "Honor Roll Students")

The diagram would identify those juniors who work after school and also receive good grades.

B. Using three finite sets, find at least two social situations in your school that can be clarified by a Venn diagram. The situations could have to do with the attributes of members of one group or of three groups. By characterizing and identifying individuals in various ways, you can find out which individuals can be put together to form a group that might not otherwise be obvious. In this way you could possibly contribute to the solving of a social problem in school.

(Continued)

Name _____

C. What group did you identify? _____

Does identifying the group help to solve a problem? _____ If so, what is the problem?

_____

_____

_____

_____

_____

_____

_____

_____

_____

_____

_____

_____

78 No Labels

A. If you were walking along an alley and happened to notice the following three containers, some distance from one another, what would you guess to be in each?

The surface is shiny and almost black, and it may be made of wood. It seems to be perforated with holes. It looks to be about 5-by-5-by-5 feet. What might be in this container?

_____
_____
_____
_____
_____

It appears to be made of glass and its outside is white. The shape is a common one for a quart container. What could be inside it?

_____
_____
_____
_____
_____
_____
_____

(Continued)

Name _____

This container appears to be made of something solid. It is brown. What might be in this container?

_____
_____
_____

B. What clues do you have about the contents of these containers by just looking at their exteriors?

dark box _____
_____
_____

white container _____
_____
_____

solid brown container _____
_____
_____

(Continued)

Name _____

What clues do you have about the contents of the three containers by looking at their surroundings?

dark box _____

_____

_____

white container _____

_____

_____

solid brown container _____

_____

_____

Does the size of the container always give you a clue as to its contents?

_____

_____

_____

_____

If the white container were lined up with three others just like it, would you make a different guess about its contents?

_____

_____

_____

_____

_____

(Continued)

C. Most containers are manufactured in standard sizes. Give three reasons why boxes, cans, bottles, and so on, are manufactured in standard sizes.

_____

_____

_____

_____

_____

Why are some bottles almost always colored brown?

_____

_____

_____

D. Draw what you think is in the box.

79 The Gopher

A. Following is a new game like soccer called "Bonzi." It is played with 11 on one side and 12 on the other side, or with 12 on one side and 13 on the other side. It's a good game to play when an uneven number of players want to play a game. The team with fewer players designates one player as its "gopher" (for "go for it"). That player gets two points for every goal scored, but he or she must be one of the defenders—usually a right back or left back. The gopher, like the goaltenders, can touch the ball with his or her hands (none of the other players can). The tendency in Bonzi is to have higher scores than in regular soccer games. Its big advantage is that when a skilled player is designated as gopher, the game can be quite exciting.

For decades baseball, basketball, and football rules went virtually unchanged. Then basketball adopted the three-point shot, and that change changed the game considerably. Even though it was unthinkable to many "purists" to change the rules for making points in basketball, the game has become even more popular.

What is your attitude about the three-point basket in basketball? Do you think there will be any more changes, such as raising the height of the basket?

_____
_____
_____
_____
_____
_____
_____

(Continued)

B. Can you think of a modification of another popular game? You might change the scoring scheme of a familiar sport. There are many ways to change the scoring system of a game. You can designate that certain players earn more points when they cross a goal with a ball or put a ball in a goal area (as is the case with Bonzi). You can give more or fewer points for certain kinds of scores. It is possible to give more weight to scores made at different times during a game. You might even develop a system in which points are lost as well as gained, as is the case with several card games.

Devise your scoring scheme for any game that might possibly benefit from a change. You can give the details of your scoring system in the space below.

80 Lucky You?

A. What is the difference between luck and chance? Is chance—or probability—just a more rational, quasiscientific way of looking at luck? At the gambling table both addicted gamblers and mathematicians trying to "break the system" experience the same events, but they use different terms for what happens to the dice, cards, and colored balls.

Which of the following events are luck and which are chance and which are something else? If one is something else, tell what it is.

1. You find a dime on the sidewalk. _____

2. You have a puncture in your car's tire; when you go out from your house to drive it, the tire is flat. _____

3. There are five candidates for a job you want, all of whom have the same experience and are the same age. You get chosen. _____

4. You win a raffle at a picnic. _____

5. Someone throws a rock at a bird and hits you instead. _____
   _____

6. A friend comes up behind you suddenly, startling you and causing you to drop your ice cream cone. _____

7. You attend a party where two or three people are sniffling; two days later you have a cold. _____

8. You are in the woods, and since it is cold you want to start a fire. Your book of matches has just a single match left, but you are able to start the fire with the one match. _____

9. You see an ad in the paper for a used bicycle at a very good price, but when you phone the advertiser, she tells you that the caller before you has bought the bicycle. _____

10. For three consecutive Saturdays it rains, and you can't have a picnic in the park that has been planned for a month. _____

(Continued)

B. Are any of the above a combination of luck and pure chance? _____
   Which ones?

   _____
   _____
   _____

   Maybe it would be a good idea to re-examine each of your answers. _____
   Did you change your mind about any of them? _____ If so, which ones?

   _____
   _____
   _____

C. Your uncle hopes that the third child his wife will have will be a boy because the first two children were girls. The baby is born a healthy and pretty girl. Your uncle is pleased, but he wonders why the third child couldn't have been a boy. How should he look upon the situation? Is it luck or probability that he should be thinking about? Explain.

   _____
   _____
   _____
   _____
   _____
   _____

Name _____

81 Educated Guesses

A. Approximately 150 people pay every day to see movies at a local theater. They each pay $7.00 for a ticket. About $25.00 in profit is derived from concessions daily. Mario, 23 and single, owns the business. If his overhead (rent, labor, electricity, and so on) is about $2,200 per day, should he hire a manager at $6.00 an hour to take his place overseeing the operation of the theater and find another job himself? He can support himself with an income of $1,300 a month if the rent on his home and food prices don't increase. If inflation is estimated to be 5 percent in the coming year, how soon will Mario have to raise his prices or find a new manager? It is now November.

You can use the space below to make your calculations.

Mario should

because _____
_____

B. Reggie rents one of the two houses he owns in town. He used to live in the house that he now rents. Before they were married, Reggie's wife told him she didn't want to live in that neighborhood, so she picked out a house she liked better in another neighborhood. Reggie thought he'd rent out his former residence. He had heard he could write off depreciation and repairs on his income tax report. Not being a particularly greedy man, Reggie decided to charge his tenants just a little more than the mortgage payments of $650 on the house (which includes his insurance), so they have a two-year lease for $675 per month.

(Continued)

Reggie lives in a town where property values are going up, however, and his property taxes for the rental have increased by 25 percent in the last year—from $960 to $1,200. This increase disturbs Reggie because he figures the benefits from owning the property as a tax break amount only to about $1,300. Moreover, the word around town is that property values will increase again next year, and he'll be paying even more property tax for his rental property. What should he do?

C. In finding answers to the problems above, you engaged in a rather common activity. Our society has many people who make a living by working on similar problems for others. What is the name of their occupation?

_____

Essentially, what does a person in that occupation do?

_____
_____
_____
_____

82 Community Fitness

A. According to a theoretical model developed by the RAND Corporation, each additional mile walked or run by a sedentary person would give him or her an additional twenty-one minutes of life and save society an average of twenty-four cents in medical and other costs. Inasmuch as health care costs have risen dramatically in the last two decades, all communities are examining fitness and preventive medicine with utmost seriousness.

Let's guess that in ten years your community decides to have an all-out campaign for fitness. Half of the sedentary people in the community (including young people) are signed up for a fitness program—and they stick to it. How much will be realized in savings to the community?

Do a little research by asking health officials and concerned citizens and determine about how many people in your community are sedentary and in need of an exercise program.

_____
_____
_____
_____
_____

B. What other implications do you see from such a campaign to improve health and lengthen life? They can affect every area of life in your community.

_____
_____
_____
_____
_____
_____
_____

Name _____

83 Relative Comfort

A. Because of his job, Frank travels to many places around the world. His business takes him to parts of Asia and Africa, as well as to the principal cities of Europe and North America. When it comes to deciding what clothes to take with him on some trips, Frank often has to play a guessing game. Even if Frank has already been to places such as Tokyo and Berne, the weather can be capricious in those cities; he might find himself dressed for wet weather and find it is hot and sultry or cold and windy. He doesn't like to travel with too much baggage, so Frank tries to restrict the number of garments he takes on his flights.

The solution to his problem, Frank believes, is to get as much information about the places he flies to as he can. Even though he usually meets with clients in air-conditioned rooms, the hotel rooms in which he stays are often without air conditioning. So, by contacting a weather service, Frank can obtain information about temperatures, humidity, and approaching storms.

Frank is about to make a trip to Asia. His stops are at Bangkok, Thailand; Kuala Lampur, Malaya; and Komatsu, Japan. He is uncertain about what weather he will encounter, but he received the following information from the weather service:

PREDICTIONS FOR FRANK'S STAYS

Bangkok—Temperature (high): 21°C; Relative Humidity: 68 percent; Skies: Cloudy; Winds: 25–35 mph; Forecast: rain, probably stormy

Kuala Lampur—Temperature (high): 24°C; Relative Humidity: 58 percent; Skies: clear; Winds: 15–25 mph; Forecast: fair

Komatsu—Temperature (high): 15°C; Relative Humidity: 62 percent; Skies: cloudy; Winds: 5–10 mph; Forecast: rain

Frank has found that the best indicator of whether he will be comfortable or not is the relative humidity reading. What do you think the conditions are like in his hotel room in each of those cities? Sketch Frank in his three hotel rooms.

(Continued)

Name _____

Bangkok

Hey! Here's your chance to become an "ARTISTO AWESOMUS"

Kuala Lampur

Komatsu

(Continued)

B. Relative humidity is the amount of water vapor in the air compared to the amount it will hold (that is, when it is saturated). The warmer the air, the more moisture it can hold. At normal atmospheric pressure, an increase in temperature of about 11°C doubles the air's moisture capacity. So, saturated air with a temperature of 18°C contains twice as much moisture as air saturated at 7°C.

Let's say that the temperature (already high) in all three cities increases by 4°C by the second day of Frank's stay. Would there be any changes in Frank's attire? How would Frank be dressed in each city? Sketch three more pictures of Frank.

Bangkok

Kuala Lampur

Komatsu

Name _____

84 Not Covered

You are just about to move into your first apartment. It's in a new and vacant apartment building at the edge of town. You are a little upset because you want a carpet on the floor before you move in your furniture. It's Thursday, and you want to have the apartment ready for a party on Saturday. The landlord has given you permission to move in tomorrow.

You'd like to have the carpet laid today. When you phone the carpet shop, they ask for dimensions. Unfortunately, you don't know and don't have a tape measure or a yardstick. What can you do? Name as many ways as you can for getting the dimensions and square footage without a tape measure or yardstick.

_____
_____
_____
_____
_____
_____
_____
_____
_____
_____

85 Ice Fishing

In northern latitudes people enjoy fishing in the winter. They put on enough warm clothes so that they won't suffer from the cold, drill holes in the ice, and drop their fishing lines. For some good reasons, these people seem to be successful in catching fish. Their success is greater in some years than in others, as is the case with all kinds of fishing.

Why don't you construct a table in which the number of fish caught is related to the hours spent ice fishing? Do a little research about ice fishing (if you don't know a lot about it now), finding out the times of the day when ice fishing is best in a state such as Minnesota. Your table can then show the number of fish caught at various hours of the day. The atmospheric conditions and the time of day are definitely factors in ocean fishing and stream fishing. Are there similar factors to be considered in ice fishing? You can check books about fishing to get the answers.

After constructing your table, make a drawing of the typical ice fishing hole; the fisherman's line, sinker, and bait; and the number of fish in the water beneath the hole. You'll have to take into consideration the ratio of the number of fish caught to the number of fish in the area beneath the hole. (How many fish are caught out of a school of thirty, for instance?)

Notes on the Units

❶ Twos and Threes

If you become especially aware of some common phenomenon, for example, red-headed people, dandelions, bottles and cans along the roadside, manhole covers, or diesel fumes, you will find yourself noting its presence more often than you had before you became highly aware of it. Here we ask your students to become aware of threes.

Your students will probably respond in a wide variety of ways. It would be enlightening for you to list at least ten threes yourself before administering this unit. Incidentally, a number of societies have regarded three as being very special. (By the way, why *are* three white balls found in front of pawn shops?)

❷ Live Numerals

This unit features personification of numerals. *We* always think of 8 as being the mother of 4 and of 9 as being the uncle of 6. That may be rather bizarre thinking on our part, but we've never been able to shake off those notions. In this unit, we go rather deeply into the idea that the numerals with which your students identify have a personality.

As far as mathematics is concerned, the questions regarding which other numerals the numeral selected by your students would associate with is intriguing. We suppose 1s and 2s and 3s must associate with each other, but do they *like* each other? Mathematicians have ideas about how numbers relate to one another that are sometimes a little mystical. Since we don't claim to be mathematicians, ours are merely whimsical.

❸ Numbering

Your students are to think seriously about numbers by giving five facts about one of the counting numbers, by reflecting about the importance of 12, and by personifying a number by relating it to a familiar individual. You can probably think of other ways for the numbers to come alive in the imaginations of your students.

Notes on the Units

4. Memorable Numbers

First, we ask your students to name some telephone numbers that use the letters corresponding to the numbers on the dial. We can recall our local symphony's number as being 54-MUSIC, for example. Then we have them devise a seven-digit number that illustrates the operations of addition and/or subtraction. We end up asking your students to identify an arithmetic progression (465-7687). The last question about devising a telephone number that demonstrates both multiplication and division is tricky. Here is an acceptable answer: 248-5469 (2 x 4 = 8) — (54 ÷ 6 = 9).

5. Numerically Speaking

This unit invites your students to personify numbers and to name numerals that belong together. (Are they compatible, friendly, or linked?) Lots of numerals go with other numerals, of course, including 1 with 2, 2 with 3, so on. With the nearly universal practice of digitalizing data, an excellent answer would be that 0 goes with the counting numbers a great deal of the time ("01" on a form, for example, so that there are two spaces to be filled). Is 0 a numeral?

6. Colorful Numerals

Some people automatically associate—or "see"—a particular color when they hear music. We're asking your students to associate colors with numerals. The questions are rather demanding and require some stretching of the imagination on the part of your students. Don't let them wriggle out of doing some genuine thinking in this unit.

7. Your Lucky Number

For millennia, people all over the world have associated good and bad luck with numbers so it would be surprising if your students hadn't picked up the notion that numbers can have special significance in their lives. Before administering the unit, ask what favorite numbers your students have. The superstitious nature of this practice is obvious, and you may or may not want to explore that aspect of lucky numbers.

8. Thirteen

We lead your students from an investigation of numbering systems to some ruminations about their personal feelings about numbers. Certain numbers may mean very little to your students, but in our culture the idea that 3, 7, or 11 is lucky is commonplace. A great many people are superstitious about 13, of course, and we bring this fact up in the unit.

The rather long introduction should serve as an adequate warm-up for the thinking that follows it. If your math program has dealt with base 5 or numbering systems other than base 10, or if you are about to introduce the subject of other numbering systems, this unit will serve as a review or a lead-in, with the added feature of bringing up superstition. Our intention is to have your students reflect upon their feelings about numbers, as well as to give them some practice in using the base 5 system. Some of your students could possibly discover for the first time that they have certain attitudes and feelings about particular numbers.

One of Torrance's eighteen constructs is "being aware of emotions." He sees emotions and feelings as playing a facilitating role in the creative process. Edward de Bono (1976) has declared that emotions are more important than anything else in thinking. He explains that emotions usually come first and then follow the thinking that is used to support the emotions. De Bono believes that even when thinking comes first the emotions give the thinking power. However, emotions are both inhibiting and facilitating, so the creative problem solver should be aware of what emotions are affecting thinking at the moment.

References

de Bono, E. 1976. *Thinking Action*. Dorset, United Kingdom: Direct Education Services.

Torrance, E. P. 1979. *The Search for Satori and Creativity*. Buffalo, N.Y.: Creative Education Foundation.

9 The Cost of Candy

The cost of candy in the future should interest your students. If the rate of increase over the past twenty-five years remains about the same, what will a candy bar cost when your students are in their thirties? Depending upon their mathematical knowledge, you can encourage your students to try two or three approaches in projecting the costs.

10 The Right Change

The idea of this unit is to persuade your students that there might be more than one explanation for the mistake—if it is indeed a mistake. Could it be that the

Notes on the Units

customer forgot about tax—or wasn't used to it since she could have come from a state that doesn't have a sales tax? Could it have been that the bar code registered the regular price but there was a sale on?

11 Symbols

Because there is very little challenge in determining what the symbols mean, emphasize the last part of the unit, which requires your students to devise symbols for a treasure hunt.

12 What Is *Your* Address?

The basic idea of the unit is that numbers can be interpreted in many ways. This activity works well when your students have been studying the decimal system, casting out nines, working with arithmetic progressions, and the like.

The example of looking at 3417 as being magical is explained, but the 1357 address is not. It is the start of an arithmetic progression, of course, and the question, "Do you consider it odd," is our attempt at a pun. The 4408 address should open your students' minds to various ways of looking at numbers.

Encourage your students to discover at least one magical address. Those with four and five digits are easier than those with only two.

13 Wrong Number

All your students should easily catch the three incorrect addition facts, and they also should have little trouble in devising an exercise such as this one. We recommend that you duplicate your students' problems or put them on an overhead or opaque projector after they have devised them.

14 Mistakes

This unit is exactly like "Wrong Number." You can have a discussion about those multiplication facts that are most troublesome (8 x 7, 9 x 6, 9 x 7, or whatever).

15 Ethiopian Multiplication

The Ethiopian method of multiplying works, but it won't be clear to your students why it works. Yes, if you reverse the columns by multiplying 14 x 19 after multiplying 19 x 14, it works just as well. The strangest part of the method

Notes on the Units

for most students will be saying 9 is half of 19. That seems to go against anyone's mathematical intuition.

16 Successive Subtraction

The challenging part of this unit comes at the end when we ask your students to think of a camping situation in which they can use successive subtraction to solve a problem. It might be for dividing food, stores, people, or time.

17 Three Problems

This is a simple exercise in identifying zero. It culminates in an invitation to make up a problem—not an easy task for many students—that has zero in it. We've given your students a good deal of latitude, so they should be able to come up with a problem similar to the ones we've given in the unit.

18 Zero

Your students are asked to apply the identity element principle to a situation in a game. A team's going scoreless in an overtime of a basketball game is an example, but there are countless occasions and situations in games when the identity element comes into play (pardon the pun).

19 What Is the Problem?

Your students will see that by subtracting the numbers in the corners from the middle number, they will get the answers found in the opposite corners of the square. The problem could be stated like this: "Place the numbers 1 through 5 in a square so that there are four answers to four subtraction combinations."

20 Fill in the Circles

Our solution:

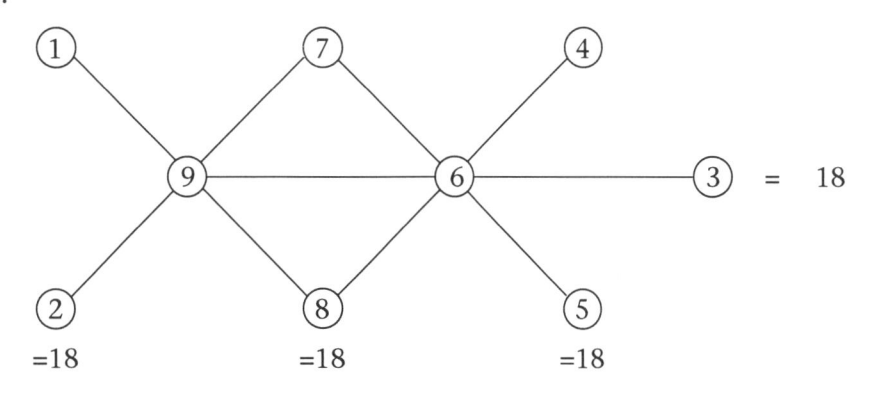

```
  (1)       (7)       (4)
     \     /   \     /
      \   /     \   /
       (9)-------(6)-------(3)  = 18
      /   \     /   \
     /     \   /     \
  (2)       (8)       (5)
  =18       =18       =18
```

147

Notes on the Units

21 More than Four Ways

In the last part of this unit, your students will have to use their imaginations. The number of 5s in an ice cream cone, for example, requires more than dividing the price of the cone by 5. It could be that the 5s are in terms of the time it takes to eat the cone (probably one or two 5s), the number of licks it takes to finish the ice cream itself, or the number of young people it might take to eat the cone when each has a bite (perhaps unsanitary but fairly realistic).

22 Two More Dollars

You can give your students practice in doing mental calculations by having them play the old Conductor game. Put one student by the side of each first desk (if your desks are arranged in rows). Try to match them approximately by their quickness in making mental calculations. When a student gets an answer before his or her fellow competitors, after you have given a series of combinations orally, he or she gets to stand next to the second seat in that row. When a student who is standing next to the last seat in the row is first to answer the next series of combinations, that student is the winner of the game. If there are twenty-five students in the class and five rows of desks, you will have five competitions so that everyone can participate. The final competition is between the five winners.

When you first play the game with a class, give three combinations and go fairly slowly. As the young people become more skilled at making mental computations, speed up and add a couple of combinations. If played regularly, the game is a wonderful way to review arithmetic facts or even facts about measurement, squaring numbers, and taking a square root. By putting students of approximately equal ability in the same competition, you will be giving each one a chance to be a winner—and if Conductor is played often, chances are all students in your class will be winners at least once in the year.

23 Tom's Game

An appropriate response to this problem requires a high degree of ingenuity. Since the experience of dividing up sides for playground games takes place so often, your students may have some clues about how to eliminate all of the waiting.

24 Tasks

If "Check your work!" is a familiar slogan in your math class, that will probably be the first thing to pop into the minds of your students when they give advice to the two impatient subjects of the stories. Other suggestions may be more revealing of the behavior and thinking of your students, and they could range from "Don't be in too much of a hurry" to "Use a calculator."

Notes on the Units

25 Sophie's Problem

You or your students may have found that your math textbook has an incorrect answer or two. Once, when our students became enthusiastic about looking for them, we found lots!

26 Ask the Right Question

Because of TV's "Jeopardy," your students know how to phrase a question after being given its answer. In this unit they will ask seven questions to elicit answers such as "in twelve hours you blink your eyes about 7,200 times." It shouldn't be too difficult for them to think of appropriate questions.

27 Find the Problem

The isosceles triangle has six squares inside and three outside, so this is our solution:

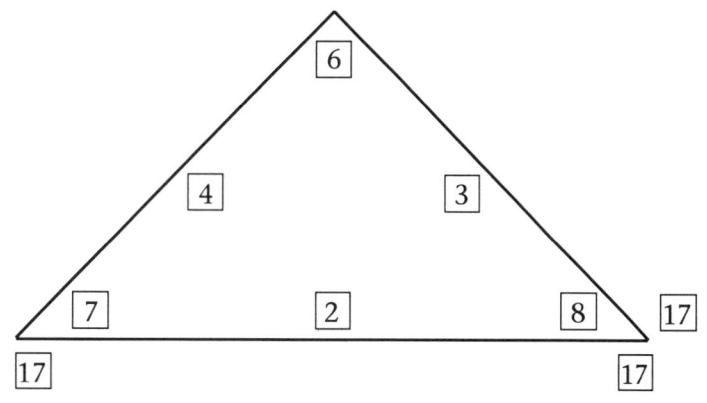

If your students see this puzzle as simply adding in three directions, they will be correct. We ask your students, however, to *verbalize* the problem. They should come up with something like this: "Without repeating a number, put any numbers in the boxes (squares) inside the triangle so that when three numbers are in a line, they add up to 17."

28 Relationships

This unit is probably the most "mathematical" of all units in the book because it has your students just think about mathematics. No real-life context is provided.

29 Planning a Colorful Event

The budgeting that this unit calls for could seem far-fetched to young people who have lavish birthday parties given to them by indulgent parents. On the other

Notes on the Units

hand, it could be more like a fantasy for those youngsters who are lucky to be fed well on their birthdays. As a lesson in fractions, however, it should suit most students.

30 Two Mistakes

Bill had an experience that is common to many of us—when one thing goes wrong, another will follow. We think your students can identify with Bill in his desire not to go to the lower floor and admit to his irate father that he went to the task completely unprepared. What can he use to measure the area in the roof to be patched? A shoelace would do. So would the span of his hand, but that wouldn't be as accurate as his shoelace. Other ideas will occur to your students.

31 Half as Much

If you have the facilities, your students can do their designing on computers or graph paper. By drawing their rooms to half scale, they will be doing some practical arithmetic along with the measuring called for in this unit.

32 Two-by-Fours

This unit is quite similar to "Half as Much." One of the principal differences is that we invite your students to design furniture itself instead of placing it in a room.

33 Hot and Deep

This unit involves your students in making conversions of Fahrenheit to Celsius and fathoms to feet. We not only ask your students to make up a problem in which someone must convert from one measure to another, but we ask them to make up another problem that can be solved in a different way. That different way could be converting one measure to another by means of a table. There are several tables for converting English measures to metric measures, for instance.

34 Enough

We invite your students to do some practical measuring—dishes being cooked, spelling marks, sleep, and television watching. The idea is to get them to appreciate the extent to which we measure things every day. We also want them to recognize that whenever we measure there are problems involved in obtaining accurate measurements.

Notes on the Units

35 Converting

This unit has to do with converting English measurements to metric measurements, but it also calls for flexibility of thinking and ingenuity on the part of the students.

36 Sea Time

Since time is such a dominant dimension in our culture, we want to encourage your students to think about how it is reckoned in two different situations. We aren't concerned if a student knows the system of bells and merely states it. Our purpose is to make your students aware of other ways of giving the time than the one they are used to.

37 Mixing Bleach

Our solution to the first problem: The proportions are one quart of bleach to six quarts of water, or 1:6. By halving the amounts and mixing one pint of bleach to six pints of water (that is, two cups of bleach and twelve cups of water), seven pints will be in the gallon container. That will leave a pint of empty space because there are eight pints to a gallon.

The solution to the second problem is found in the fact that the container is clear. Because of its shape, any measuring device (a piece of string doubled on itself, for instance) can be used to mark the $1/4$, $1/2$, $3/4$, and $7/8$, levels on the outside of the container. One pint of bleach and six pints of water will bring the mixture up to the $7/8$ mark.

38 Geometric Artistry

This unit can be used as a combination art and math exercise if you think it will be interesting to your students. Collages with geometric shapes of various colors can be a satisfying activity in the midst of a math lesson or vice versa.

39 Shapes

Your students may recall those early handwriting lessons that featured circles and straight lines. If so, this unit will be something of a review.

Notes on the Units

40 Concentric Squares?

One of the perceptions most people have of the concentric squares on the left is that the one on top is larger than the one below it (and, of course, it isn't) because of the larger square inside the bottom figure.

41 Figuring

By our reckoning, there are a total of ten triangles in the first figure. We think there are thirteen rectangles in the second figure, but we could be wrong.

42 Geometric Flooring

The technical name for the skill required in this unit is "figural redefinition." By using some lines and ignoring others, the student should be able to see eight rectangles in the tile pattern. In the second figure, there are fourteen triangles, five squares, eight isosceles triangles, and nine rectangles (by our reckoning).

43 Frames and Panes

A lot of drawing is required in this unit, so it would be a good idea if your students had graph paper on which to do it. If they have access to computers, they can do their drawings in that way.

44 A New Route

This unit calls for a practical application of fundamental algebraic principles. The critical point in this problem is determining where those two shortcuts were that Norm can't take anymore. We might guess that they are where he went from the second to the third house and then from the third to the fourth house, but that isn't stated in the problem.

45 A Gem of an Idea

The drawing of a three-dimensional object is becoming available to students through computer technology, but we expect your students to draw the hexagonal and tretragonal crystals in the traditional two-dimensional way. The really interesting part of this activity is producing the "unusual and beautiful" colors for the gems.

46 Mowing 'Em Down

Depending upon climate, terrain, and type of grass, there are recommended ways of mowing lawns, but the one variable that the experts take into consideration if they alter a pattern of mowing is the slope of the lawn. We recommend a class discussion following this unit; there will be differences of opinion as to how to cut the grass efficiently.

47 Kitchen Design

This unit can perhaps call forth some ingenious thinking on the part of would-be architects, product designers, and home economists. If a student doesn't have access to a kitchen, you might provide pictures from one or more of the magazines that feature home interiors.

48 Going Around

Your students will be best served if they can manipulate objects when attempting to come up with answers to the questions posed in this unit.

49 Count the Ways

If asking for four hypotheses is unrealistic for your class, ask for two or three. There are quite a few alternative routes and quite a few explanations for why the four students take varying amounts of time to get to school. Is there a reason that the senior takes the least amount of time and the freshman the greatest? We imagine your students are experts concerning this subject and masters of dawdling, hurrying, shortcutting, circumventing, and avoiding.

50 What's the Angle?

The mathematical problem in this unit is very basic geometry, but the practical problem of where Mr. Jasper will find an instrument to measure the angle is more challenging. In the story we mention Mr. Jasper's son's protractor, but actually a ruler would do in using the method of similar triangles.

51 Configurations

This unit's thrust is to encourage your students to combine geometric shapes, an activity that is seriously practiced in countless commercial, scientific, and artistic enterprises. It is meant to be a relaxed, playful unit, one in which your students can experiment and discover.

Notes on the Units

52 Parts

There are just two parts to this unit: determining what the common element is in the five questions about fractions and devising three similar questions dealing with the same topic. The second part will be the challenge.

53 Equal Parts

The obvious solution to the problem is that James himself represents the fourth fifth-grader, thus giving his class the required one-third. However, your students are asked to find *two other* solutions. One solution (not a good one) is to have James direct the operation and have one third-grader and one fourth-grader drop out. What do you think the third solution is? Write to us if you and your students can't come up with an answer.

54 Percentage Baseball

To raise its winning percentage the team has to win its next two games. We worked it out using algebra, but your students can arrive at the answer in other ways.

55 Tracy Figures

The obvious advice for Tracy is the same as for everyone else, that is, make sure your outgo doesn't exceed your income. Tracy should budget.

56 Sprouts

There are at least three ways to express success and failure in mathematical terms. The success rate can be expressed as a fraction ($^{20}/_{25}$ and $^{4}/_{5}$), a percentage (80 percent), or a decimal fraction (.80). The rate of failure can be expressed as a fraction ($^{5}/_{25}$, $^{1}/_{5}$), a percentage (20 percent), or a decimal fraction (.20).

You could also say that someone won or succeeded 3 times as often as she lost, or at a ratio of 3:1. That means a percentage of 75 or .75.

57 Twice as Much

You can substitute other commonplace ratios for the seven we have offered. Possible topics: amount of television viewing to total free time at home; proportion of brown-eyed students in the classroom; proportion of students wearing black shoes in the classroom; proportion of students who have bicycles.

Notes on the Units

58 Getting Smaller

Some good could come out of your students' completing this unit. We invite them to devise two strategies for dealing with an item's becoming smaller (at the same price as formerly) and for coping with a rise in the price of an item.

59 More Stop than Go

This unit involves your students in the kind of rudimentary research that people conduct regarding their everyday problems. The question we pose—are there enough data to come to a reasonably valid conclusion about the bias in the way the traffic signals are set?—is the one you will want to zero in on if there is a discussion of this unit in class.

60 How's the Weather Up There?

It is unlikely that the human race will continue to produce individuals who exceed seven feet at the same rate we have seen in the past thirty years or so. What should be interesting to your students is the tremendous height that basketball players will attain fifty years from now if the rate of growth remains constant. Your students will probably find that diet is one of the most important factors in the increased height of people such as the Japanese. If you allow enough time, this unit could prove rich in learning experiences.

61 The Puddlejumpers and Puffers Parade

Road races are popular all over the country (and the world). "The Puddlejumpers and Puffers Parade" is fictional, but it is also fairly typical of races that are sponsored in many small communities. There are many ways of rewarding finishers, and we must confess that there is usually no grousing among the officials as to how to hand out prizes. Our intention is simply to encourage your students to think about alternatives. The first question posed in the unit can be answered by simply using this equation to find the number of participants in Group C: $4n + 3n + n = 152$. There were 19 participants in Group C, so there were 57 in Group B.

62 Less than $10.00

You will probably be interested in the ways your students interpret the calculations. Whether they will buy the idea that people use algebra in their everyday lives is conjectural. They may be skeptical, but we actually use simple algebra quite often.

Notes on the Units

63 Multiple Distributions

Of all the units, "Multiple Distributions" requires the most resourcefulness. Experienced teachers of beginning algebra would be challenged by it, but perhaps your students have some insights that wouldn't occur to most teachers about how to get the law across.

64 Nine Left

Whether anyone would write out an algebra problem in such a neat fashion is conjectural. At any rate, your students can try to interpret the figures. Our guess is that 75 steers were sold in the month of April, or would have been if all the steers had been sold at the monthly auction. At that rate, 900 would be sold in a year's time. However, since 9 steers weren't sold at the auction, the man could expect 834 steers to be sold in the next eleven months if the average of 75 steers sold holds up. There can be other interpretations, of course.

65 Story Problems

Perhaps students hate story problems because they are naturally lazy. When a story problem is to be solved, the student must make some decisions about what is called for, and that means there must be some genuine thinking. In this unit, the thinking is provoked by our asking your students to create a story problem to fit the algorism, $x - 1/3x = 64 + 12$. In a way, creating a story problem is a good deal more difficult than just solving a story problem. The problem has the advantage, however, of pointing out the practical nature of mathematics.

66 The Sketch

In a four-square game, the server is in the "A" square, and the players progress from "D" to "A" as errors are made and players are eliminated. We suggest that your students modify the sketch, if they wish, and create their own game with our sketch as the basis.

67 It Figures

This unit is designed to encourage your students to become more aware of the importance of mathematics in their lives. We expect students to investigate how various workers use mathematics to make decisions as to which workers need more math. Allow enough time for your students to dig into the unit.

68 Four Plus Seven Make Nine

This puzzle is most easily solved if the student is able to guess when the four-minute timer is halfway finished, but we tell your students that that can't be done. Here is our solution:

1. Start both timers. At the end of four minutes the four-minute timer will be finished and the seven-minute timer will have three minutes left. Elapsed time: four minutes.

2. As soon as the four-minute timer is finished, turn both timers over immediately. When three minutes have transpired, the seven-minute timer will be finished, but the four-minute timer will have one minute left. Elapsed time: three minutes.

3. Turn the timers over quickly and let the four-minute timer finish. There will be only one minute gone from the seven-minute timer. Elapsed time: one minute.

4. Turn over the seven-minute timer. Only one minute had elapsed for it, so when the seven-minute timer is finished one minute more will have elapsed. Elapsed time: one minute. Total elapsed time: nine minutes.

If you have two egg timers for four and seven minutes (which we understand is most unlikely) you can demonstrate the solution.

69 Mel Comes Through

It should be fascinating to learn how your students will try to solve Mel's problem. If there is a resource room, Mel can seek help there, but most schools don't have that advantage. He can go to the library as well, but what will he find there? He might even go to the principal if the principal is good at helping children with learning problems. There are other steps that young people can take that genuinely help them learn. We are presuming that Mel, unfortunately, doesn't want to go to his teacher for some reason.

70 How Do You Poach a Roach?

Here are some possible answers to a few of the most perplexing questions:

- Someone might use a counting device (a clicker) to count the sheep coming through a stile in order to "meter a bleater."
- To "curve a nerve," a physician or medical technician can plot the reaction of a nerve to a stimulus on a graph.
- The flight of a lark can be plotted on paper or on a computer in order to "arc a lark."

Notes on the Units

- The most satisfactory way to "compound a mound" is to put a pile of money in the bank and have it earn compound interest.
- If you take turns with someone in riding a pony or a horse, you'll be "dividing a ride."
- The last question—"How do you half (halve) a calf without harming it?"—may not be a good question for a butcher. We suggest you weigh it and divide by two.

71 A Square Inch

Since this unit deals with freckles, it may or may not have relevance for some of your students. A bit of humor is implicit in the unit, but your students are asked to be involved in sampling techniques and biases, and it is therefore a valuable exercise in learning about the procedures of polling that affect American politics to a surprising extent.

72 Calculating by Hand

After giving examples of the use of division on the playground and during a "normal day," your students are asked to think of all of the ways they can use a hand calculator. We suggest that you have a class discussion of this unit following its completion.

73 Yebas for Dollars

"Yebas for Dollars" is a unit about monetary systems and can be integrated with a social studies unit. Money is always a topic of importance because the shifting values of a dollar, a pound, a mark, and a yen have direct consequences upon the world's economy. Your students can reassess the value of a dollar by examining the power of the yeba.

74 Back to the Basics

There have been several scares concerning viruses afflicting computers worldwide, and there will likely be more. Computers aren't the only tools of mathematicians, of course. Ask your students if any other catastrophe would affect mathematicians as much or more.

75 Experimenting with Humor

We're not sure if your students will think the two jokes are funny. On the other hand, the little experiment is a deadly serious assignment, and, if they get involved in the activity, your students can learn a good deal about polling and a little about statistics.

76 Profits

Merchants only wish they could predict their sales accurately in any season of the year. We picked the fall because December is so crucial to the year's profits that its value is disproportionate to the rest of the year.

77 It's Easy Venn You Know How

Venn diagrams are being used more frequently now because of the increasing importance of logic as a result of the dominance of computers in all phases of society.

78 No Labels

We don't want to encourage your students to snoop, but guessing what is inside a container is natural. The "What's in the Box?" activity would be a good way to introduce this unit. Have students take turns guessing the contents in a nondescript box about the size of a hat box. You can put marbles, beebees, hairpins, golf balls, marshmallows, coins, pencils, an apple, a tangerine, keys, bread crusts, or any number of other things inside the box. Students can shake the box, smell the contents, or do anything except open it in order to get clues. Make them do some genuine thinking.

79 The Gopher

Scoring systems are as necessary as the balls, pucks, horseshoes, chalk, and other equipment that we use in our games. Although rules are often debated, scoring systems must remain constant during games or the games will become chaotic. Scoring in basketball was changed only after long study, debate, and careful scrutiny. Scoring in football hasn't changed since its earliest days. Nevertheless, we invite your students to modify the scoring system of a popular game. If they need some suggestions, you might offer such games as Steal the Bacon, horseshoes, anagrams, tic-tac-toe, or jacks.

Notes on the Units

80 Lucky You?

This unit is only an introduction to probability. Actually, there are only three instances given in the unit where probability, and not luck, obtain: the raffle at the picnic; the likelihood of rain on three consecutive Saturdays; and the uncle's having a third daughter. (One of the most common beliefs, and one that is hard to dispel, is that the third child is more likely to be a son when the first two are daughters.)

81 Educated Guesses

Your students are going to be affected by the business world, so this unit is one that will have some relevance to their lives now and in the future. We present two ordinary business situations and ask your students to make some decisions. In effect, students are to act as if they are accountants, in a simplified way.

82 Community Fitness

For the past decade or so physical fitness has been a prime topic of concern in the nation. At this writing, however, reports that young people are less fit than were their parents and grandparents at the same ages disconcert health professionals. We suggest that your students take this unit seriously and actually investigate the fitness of their community.

83 Relative Comfort

Young people with short attention spans will have to be coaxed or prodded to get through this unit. We hope that the idea of travel, however, will encourage them to persist in doing the reading and reacting and then the thinking and calculating called for in "Relative Comfort." Travel ties in nicely with social studies and science units.

84 Not Covered

Some students could be members of families that have recently moved, so this unit is not as far-fetched as it might seem. Your students should be able to come up with three or four ways to estimate the square footage of the floor to be carpeted. If they know the length of a shoe, they can pace of the dimensions; similarly, if they know the lengths of their strides with some certainty, they can make a rough estimate of the dimensions. If the length of a belt is given on the inside (as it often is), students can use the belt. Most of us have a fairly accurate estimate of our reach, but using our reach would be a clumsy way of measuring the floor. One of your clever students will wonder why borrowing a tape measure from someone in the apartment building wouldn't be the best way of all!

85 Ice Fishing

We recommend this unit in cases where students are interested in fishing. It may be boring to young people who have little interest in that pastime. The part that intrigues us most is the time of day (or night) when ice fishing is best. Is ice fishing like stream fishing in that time of day, weather conditions, and bait (lures) are important factors in landing fish? There is a good deal of information about these questions that is readily available to your students.

Look to these books by Robert Myers to give your students problem-solving skills to last a lifetime!

WHAT NEXT?
Futuristic Scenarios for Creative Problem Solving
by Robert E. Myers and E. Paul Torrance
Grades 6–12

Tap into students' natural interest in the future with writing activities you can incorporate into language arts, social studies, or humanities programs.

Select from 52 exciting units to nourish creative thinking and to inspire thinking about the future. Each unit includes an overview, warm-up topics, suggestions for presentation, and writing exercise.

388 pages, 8½" x 11", softbound

1049-W . . . $29

FACING THE ISSUES
Creative Strategies for Probing Critical Social Concerns
by Robert E. Myers
Grades 6–12

Involve your students with 52 units that encourage them to think independently, deeply, and imaginatively while grappling with current social issues.

Each unit contains a brief teacher's section to help you get started. You'll also have reproducible student sheets to use as springboards for discussions or for recording individual responses.

256 pages, 8½" x 11", softbound

1053-W . . . $30

CALL, WRITE, OR FAX FOR YOUR FREE CATALOG!

ORDER FORM
☎ Please include your phone number in case we have questions about your order.

Qty.	Item #	Title	Unit Price	Total
	1049-W	What Next?	$29	
	1053-W	Facing the Issues	$30	

Name _____
Address _____
City _____
State _____ Zip _____
Phone (_____) _____

Method of payment (check one):
❏ Check or Money Order ❏ Visa
❏ MasterCard ❏ Purchase Order attached
Credit Card No. _____
Expires _____
Signature _____

Subtotal
Sales Tax (AZ residents, 5%)
S & H (10% of Subtotal-min $3.00)
Total (U.S. Funds only)

CANADA: add 22% for S & H and G.S.T.

100% SATISFACTION GUARANTEE

Upon receiving your order you'll have 30 days of risk-free evaluation. If you are not 100% satisfied, return your order within 30 days for a 100% refund of the purchase price. No questions asked!

To order write or call:

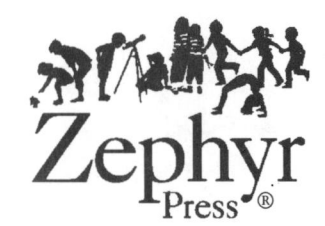

Zephyr Press®

REACHING THEIR HIGHEST POTENTIAL

P.O. Box 66006-W
Tucson, AZ 85728-6006

(520) 322-5090
FAX (520) 323-9402